What Others are Saying about Get Real!

Do you want the Bible to come alive? Do you want it to be real? Do you want to align your life to its truths? Experience **Get Real!** as it explores the life of Ruth, who battles many of the same issues young women face today: self-esteem, friends, suffering, purity, guys, and much more. Penetrating questions invite you to wrestle with truth as it relates to these tough issues. Rebecca and her teen daughter Danya creatively bridge the gap between the cultures by candidly sharing their stories of how God worked in and through their lives just as He did with Ruth. Want to go deeper? **Get Real!**

Nancy Butkowski
Author and Speaker for *FamilyLife*

"If you're looking for a contemporary resource that equips girls to live authentically in a bogus world, then **Get Real!** is it! Godly wisdom, inspiring truths, and transforming applications are captured on every page. Like a spiritual key, this youth-friendly Bible study will unlock your teen's desire to live for God in a real way. As an added bonus, Rebecca's daughter, Danya, shares weekly about her own walk of faith. I not only highly recommend it, but I'm getting one for my own daughter!"

Micca Campbell
Author and Speaker for *Proverbs 31 Ministries*

"Rebecca Ingram Powell has done it again! With an undeniable gift for reaching the hearts of teens, she has created a rich, intriguing study of God's Word that is sure to ignite a deeper, more intimate relationship with Christ. Girls, if you liked **Wise Up!** you'll absolutely love **Get Real!**"

Ginger Plowman
Author, *Don't Make Me Count to Three!* and *Heaven at Home*

GET REAL!

Embrace the Reality of Ruth

Rebecca Ingram Powell

ISBN 13: 978-1-4141-0952-7
ISBN 10: 1-4141-0952-0
Library of Congress Catalog Card Number: 2007922410

This book is lovingly dedicated to my husband,
Richard Alan Powell

I will go wherever you go and live wherever you live. Your people will be my people, and your God will be my God. I will die where you die and will be buried there. May the LORD punish me severely if I allow anything but death to separate us!

Ruth 1:16-17

TABLE OF CONTENTS

Week Six

Week Seven

Week Eight

Week Nine

Welcome to **Get Real! Embrace the Reality of Ruth.** I am so excited to have you join me in this Bible study! The drama of the book of Ruth plays out like the script of an Academy Award-winning film. Many scholars claim it is the best short story ever written. Although Ruth suffered many losses and great hardship in her life, she continued to pursue God. Her intriguing story chronicles the real life of a woman who wanted God more than she wanted anything else. In seeking Him first, she got everything else she wanted and needed. He gave her the desires of her heart.

The Word of God is real. It is powerful. It is a letter written to you by the One who knows you best and loves you most. I encourage you to use a Bible translation you find easy to understand. Throughout this study, I have mostly used the New International Version (NIV) and the New Living Translation (NLT), along with Eugene Petersen's paraphrase, *The Message,* as an additional resource. Most Bible translations are freely available online at various sites, including www.Crosswalk.com and www.BibleGateway.com.

Let me share with you the special features of this study.

Read the Script

Get Real! Embrace the Reality of Ruth begins each day with a Bible reading. Monday, Tuesday, and Wednesday of each week, you will be reading a few verses from the book of Ruth. Occasionally there will be an additional passage to read. Please don't hurry through the Scripture reading in order to get to the story in the lesson. What you read in God's Word is much more important than anything I have to say.

Journaling

At the end of each day's lesson, you will find several questions with space for journaling your thoughts. These questions are included as a way for you to process what you have learned. They are formulated in a way that will stir your heart toward deeper conversations with God and a closer relationship with Him. Meeting with you every day is the Lord's desire! He is looking forward to the time the two of you will share as you trek through the pages of Ruth.

Picture This

On Thursdays, the study will turn to New Testament passages as we look at the seven I AM sayings of Christ found in the book of John. These passages connect incredibly with our Old Testament study in Ruth.

Take Two

Every Friday, the lessons are written by my fifteen-year-old daughter, Danya. You will enjoy her *Reality Check* as she speaks to your heart from hers. You can read more about Danya on page 163.

Appendices

Tucked away at the back of this book are three special sections that include things I just couldn't leave out!

APPENDIX A - PRAYER: YOUR BACKSTAGE PASS A very important part of this Bible study is prayer. You will be praying for a Mahlon, a Naomi, an Orpah, a Ruth, and your own Boaz each week of this study. Prayer changes things! Every time you speak to God, He hears you. Through this study, you will learn to pray for others.

APPENDIX B - SCRIPTURISTICS: THE NAME GAME This appendix includes some extra info on the importance the Israelites placed on people's names. You'll be asked to read this section on Wednesday of Week One. Carve out some extra time for this because it is vitally important for understanding key elements in the book of Ruth. Also, because Scripture memory is essential to a growing Christian life, I am asking you to commit to memorizing a fairly chunky-sized passage in Ruth. You have four to choose from, and they are listed here.

APPENDIX C - YOU'RE ISRAELITES, AREN'T YOU? by Dr. Ralph F. Wilson. This fictional re-telling of the story of Rahab has been included with Dr. Wilson's permission. You'll be asked to read this section on Tuesday of Week Five.

Before the curtain goes up, before the actors are cast, before the director is assigned, it starts with a story. God wrote Ruth's story. His heart provided the stage, His hands formed the set, and His hope conceived the Hero. My prayer is that through this study, you, like Ruth, will come to know the One who wrote your story: the beginning and the end and everything that happens in between.

COMING UP NEXT

WELCOME TO THE SHOW

Monday
LIGHTS! CAMERA! ACTION!
AN INTRODUCTION

Tuesday
LAW & ORDER
BEHIND THE SCENES

Wednesday
SURVIVOR
AND THEN THERE WAS ONE

Thursday
PICTURE THIS
PICTURE PERFECT—WHAT DOES JESUS LOOK LIKE?

Friday
TAKE TWO
REALITY CHECK WITH DANYA: ME

LIGHTS! CAMERA! ACTION!

Read the Script
Psalm 119:97-105

AN INTRODUCTION

When I'm with my friend Ginger, I never know what to expect.

This time, we were racing madly down the streets of New York City, weaving in and out of people as fast as our feeble legs and full stomachs could take us. Ginger had purchased tickets for us to see the Broadway production of *Beauty and the Beast,* and as we were savoring our last bites of cheesecake after a huge lunch on the other side of the city, she realized she did not have the tickets with her. We would have to grab the tickets at our hotel before heading over to the theater. A quick look at the time indicated if we detoured to pick up the tickets, we would never make the opening curtain. Ginger was worried because she had heard that the ushers would not let latecomers in the theater, so as not to disrupt others. Then again, we knew they would not let us in at all if we didn't have the tickets. So off we went.

After two subway changes and a mad tear through Times Square, we finally arrived at the theater. With all the charm of her southern drawl, Ginger breathlessly explained our mishap to a smiling usher. As we handed him the tickets, he graciously agreed to let us go inside between scenes. With his help, we hastily found our seats in the large auditorium, lit only by the tiniest sub lights on the floor and along the walls. Within seconds the heavy black stage curtains opened, the spotlights spilled through the darkness, and the colorful stage resonated with life, drama, and song. It was like a humongous hand had picked us up off the busy street outside and dropped us into the middle of another world.

--- ★ ---

That is very much how you might feel when you begin reading the Bible.[1] The times and the culture of the ancient lands are so different from the world we live in. It is as though we pick up God's precious Word and His humongous hand drops us into the middle of another world. The truth of the matter, however, is while the world has changed, people are very much the same. That's the reality of the book of Ruth. Centuries ago, fashion, architecture, and lifestyles were quite different. But people, with their laughter, loneliness, and longings, were much the same. The Bible reaches people's hearts because although times change, people don't. God never changes. His Word is amazing. He uses it constantly to bring us into right relationship with Him.

God never changes. His Word is amazing. He uses it constantly to bring us into right relationship with Him.

--- ★ ---

In order to understand how much the Bible has to say to you, as a 21st Century teen—a young woman!—you must learn to do more than read it. You've got to learn how to study it.

When I was in college, my friend Jennie was always studying her Bible. She literally loved God's Word, devouring it daily. I knew something was missing from my spiritual life because I did not have that same desire for the Scriptures. So one day, I simply asked her, "Jennie, how did you get to the point where you love God's Word so much?"

She smiled and replied, "For almost a year now, my daily prayer request has been this: *Lord, make Your Word like candy to me, where I love its taste and cannot get enough of it.*"

Have you ever thought about the Bible being something you can't get enough of? A book you just can't put down? Like candy you keep sneaking back for more of?

Sandwiched between the Old Testament books of Judges and 1 Samuel rests the book of Ruth. Thumbing through the Bible, its four chapters are easy to miss; they are nearly buried by the violent days of the judges on one side and the dramatic history of Israel's monarchy on the other.

Ruth is a pause.

Ruth is a picture.

Ruth is a prompt—our cue that on the other side of the battles and the brawls, the kings and the commanders, there were people living their lives. There were families and friends. There were losses and loves. There was ruin. And there was romance. Ruth is a story of everyday life. As you open your Bible, within seconds God's Holy Spirit will spill across the pages, opening your heart to a colorful stage resonating with life, drama, and song. Let's go behind the scenes to another world, where you never know what to expect!

JOURNALING

- What three words describe your attitude when it comes to Bible study?

  ____

- How would your life be different if you loved God's Word as much as you loved your favorite food?

  ____

  ____

- What are you willing to do in order to make loving God's Word a priority in your life?

  ____

____

____

🎬 Which verse stands out from your Scripture reading today? Write it here.

____

____

____

____

🎬 Read Appendix A. Pray for the *Mahlon* you know today.

🎬 Will you commit to pray Jennie's prayer over the next nine weeks of this study? If you
will, make a record of your commitment below. *Lord, make Your Word like candy to me, where
I love its taste and cannot get enough of it.*

____

____

LAW AND ORDER

Read the Script
Judges 2:8-23

BEHIND THE SCENES

The book of Ruth, as you will see tomorrow, begins with an unforgettable phrase: "In the days when the judges ruled…" When you think of "judges," you probably think of someone who sits in a court of law and rules with a gavel in hand. When the Bible talks about judges, however, it speaks of a time in history when judges ruled Israel.

After Moses died, Joshua took over leadership of the Hebrew nation. Eventually Joshua passed on as well. Both Moses and Joshua had been great leaders who were constantly pointing the Israelites to God, reminding them of the great things God had done for them and urging them to worship Him alone. The Bible explains, "The people worshiped God throughout the lifetime of Joshua and the time of the leaders who survived him, leaders who had been in on all of God's great work that He had done for Israel."[2] Once all those individuals died, however, their shoes were filled by a generation that did not know the Lord and did not know about the great things He had done. Those were difficult days for Israel. They were caught up in a cycle of disobedience that flooded their lives with pain and chaos time after time, generation after generation. The path of sin always led to the same result: God's judgment.

A cycle has a definite pattern that produces the same result. Have you ever studied the water cycle? The circulation of the earth's water supply is an ongoing sequence of natural events: Precipitation (rain/snow/sleet) falls. It waters the ground and then drains into creeks, lakes, and rivers, flowing out to sea. The sun's heat causes evaporation, forming invisible water vapor. Rising, the vapor cools and forms clouds. Precipitation falls, and we are back at the cycle's beginning. The same path leads to the same result, time after time.

As you read in today's passage, the Israelites were following the same path as well, and always, it led to the same result.

--★--

It's pretty easy to get caught up in a sin cycle.

--★--

1.   They did evil in the eyes of the Lord. Their sin included abandoning the God of Israel and bowing down to the false Baal-gods of their enemies, causing the Lord to become angry toward them.

2.   God then handed them over to their enemies. They became an oppressed people, slaves under the authority of enemy nations—depressed and defeated.

3.   Once they realized the mess they were in, they cried out to the Lord to save them.

4.   In His mercy, God raised up a judge to lead the people back into *right relationship* (based on obedience to His Lordship) with Him. But ultimately, like Moses and Joshua, that human judge died. With no leadership, the Israelites returned to their evil ways and arrived back at the cycle's beginning.

It's pretty easy to get caught up in a sin cycle. You might even find yourself in one right now. Lindsey* is trapped in a sin cycle of gossip. Whenever she hangs around with Sonia, they start talking about other people. Lindsey knows it's wrong to gossip, and she always asks forgiveness afterwards. Lindsey is smart enough to know if Sonia talks to *her* about *other people,* odds are Sonia talks to *other people* about *her.* But the next time she sees Sonia, she falls right back into the sin. It seems as though she can't help herself, although she knows there are plenty of other things to talk about. Lindsey knows God's forgiveness is real, but lately, something doesn't seem quite right in her relationship with Him.

Behind the scenes of the drama in Ruth was a sinful nation who rebelled against God, got into trouble, and cried out for His help, over and over. God sent judges to help His people find the way back to a right relationship with Him, but the judges were only human. They had faults, phobias, and fears. The only way to bridge the gap between God and people was through a divine Redeemer, one who was without sin. That's Jesus. He was the promised Redeemer, symbolized throughout Ruth in the character of Boaz. But I'm getting a little ahead of myself!

The Bible explains that God is faithful and just to forgive us our sins and cleanse us from all unrighteousness,[3] but forgiveness only comes with repentance. Repentance means you truly regret the wrong you have done, not because you got caught or because you are being punished for it, but because you understand that you sinned. Your sin separates you from God. Because you love Him so much and you have a glimpse of His great love for you through Jesus Christ, you resolve not to continue in your sin. You turn away from it. You do not go back to it. If you recognize a sin cycle in your life today, surrender it to God.

JOURNALING

A sin cycle is easy to spot in others, but sometimes not so easy to identify in ourselves. Read Ephesians 5:1-4, asking God to show you where you are trapped by sin. Acknowledge that sin before God by writing it down here.

____

____

____

■ Now repent. Turn away from that sin. Ask for God's forgiveness and His help in breaking the sin cycle in your life. Write your prayer here.

____

____

____

____

____

____

____

■ Copy Galatians 5:1 in the space below.

____

____

____

■ Turn to page 151 and pray for the *Naomi* you know today.

SURVIVOR

Read the Script
Ruth 1:1-5

AND THEN THERE WAS ONE

I don't know what it is like to be really hungry.

I have dieted. I have skipped meals as a matter of convenience. On different occasions, I have fasted. In all these instances, however, I did without as a matter of choice. Food has always been available.

In today's Scripture reading, Elimelech, Naomi's husband, was confronted with the harsh reality of a *famine*. That is a scary word. It means there was a severe shortage of food in the land of Bethlehem. Interestingly, the word "Bethlehem" means *house of bread*. Bethlehem was God's Promised Land—the land flowing with milk and honey. Yet at this time, there was no provision there. Famines were not unusual in Palestine. In fact, the region suffered from famines often, as their crops were dependent upon a certain amount of rainfall. Still, some Bible scholars believe the famine was sent as a punishment on Israel. Remember yesterday's lesson and the cycle of sin. Some people believe the story of Ruth takes place during the judgeship of Gideon. They think this particular season of famine was God's tool to draw the people back to Him. Whatever the case, the food supply was scarce, and there was much suffering.

Elimelech decided to take his family and ride out the famine from the more fertile land of Moab. *Moab?* Wait just a minute! Throughout Israel's history, Moab was a recurrent enemy, oppressing the Hebrew people and opposing Jehovah God. Evidently, there must have been a season of peace—or at least toleration—between the two countries at this time. To be honest, I'm not sure why Elimelech took his family there. Twice in the first two verses, the author of Ruth mentions the fact that Elimelech is from Bethlehem, but he is going to live in Moab! The repetition here emphasizes the shock value. This is hard to believe. Why would an Ephrathite[4] leave the Promised Land to go to Moab? What was he thinking? The Bible does express that in Elimelech's mind, this was a temporary fix. He did not intend to make a permanent move to this heathen land of the Moabites. After all, they were Israel's enemy, a people of many gods and excessive idol worship.

Desperate times can lead people to do things they might not normally do. Elimelech's family was prosperous. He could afford to pull up stakes and flee the famine. Other families had no choice. They did what they

Why would an Ephrathite leave the Promised Land to go to Moab? What was he thinking?

had to do to stay alive, and some did not make it. Some Bible scholars have suggested that Elimelech fled to Moab merely to sustain his higher standard of living. They believe his actions reflect a spirit of discontent, not to mention a shallow faith. Why not rest in God's country, believing on Him to move on behalf of His people? Why journey to enemy territory, even for a short time? But I don't want to be too hard on Elimelech. It could be he did not think his sickly boys, Mahlon and Kilion,[5] would be able to survive the ordeal of a famine.

Elimelech, however, was the one to die first. The Bible does not state the cause of his death. His passing made Naomi a widow, but she still had her sons. They married Moabite women, Ruth and Orpah. Sadly, as the book of Ruth begins, Mahlon and Kilion have both died as well. Naomi's personal tragedy of widowhood was now multiplied to excess.

JOURNALING

- Perhaps you and your family have suffered tragedy in your lives. Can you identify with Naomi's sorrow? How? Use this space to describe how you imagine Naomi must have felt after losing everything.

____

____

____

____

____

____

- Do you think Elimelech made the right choice in leaving Bethlehem because of the famine? Why or why not?

____

____

____

- Turn to page 152 and pray for the *Ruth* you know today.

- Before we go any further in our study of *Ruth,* you will need to spend some time reading Appendix B: *Scripturistics.*

PICTURE PERFECT

Read the Script
Isaiah 53:1-9

WHAT DOES JESUS LOOK LIKE?

I love pictures. I love taking them, and I love putting them in scrapbooks and albums. I love framed pictures of family and friends hanging on the walls of my home and settled on dresser tops. Pictures tell stories. They remind us of good times and special events. A picture is like having a piece of someone. It's something you can hang on to. I love that!

Since we don't have the luxury of a photograph of Jesus, what do you think He looks like? There are innumerable artists' renditions of Christ, scores of drawings and paintings in every kind of medium imaginable. Art gives us a chance to express what we think Jesus looks like. Art is personal like that. Your own special creativity allows you to put your feelings into form and to give your thoughts a life of their own. Art is something you can hang on to!

My friend Stephen S. Sawyer is an artist. He paints beautiful, breath-taking pictures of Christ. He calls his collection of Jesus pictures, "Art for God."[6] The majority of paintings in the *Art for God* collection depict Jesus in the traditional dress of His day. It's the few that don't that spark some controversy. Most people already have a picture in their minds of what Jesus looks like, and they really don't want anyone to mess around with it! But Steve says candidly, "I paint somebody who's alive. If you know somebody who's alive today, you're going to portray them the way you see them today. I wasn't there two thousand years ago, but He's alive and well today, and that's really the Jesus I'm painting." Knowing somebody implies a relationship—a significant, personal connection between two people.

When I met my husband's friends, Jeff and Brian, identical twins, I could not tell them apart. I avoided calling them by name because I didn't know who was who! But as I spent time with these two young men, developing friendships with each of them, they no longer looked alike to me. They were totally separate people with distinct personalities, styles, and expressions. The relationship made all the difference.

Even if we had a photo of Jesus, it would never substitute for a real relationship with Him. Holding a picture in your hand doesn't mean you *know* a person. After all, there are plenty of famous celebrities and historical figures I recognize because I know what they look like. But I do not really know them.

Jesus wants you to know Him.

Picture this: Jesus wants you to know Him. And because He knew no picture would ever do Him justice, He didn't leave behind a snapshot

---

of Himself when He lived in a human body on this planet. He left us with His word: God's Holy Word. In the book of John, Jesus used several wonderfully descriptive phrases to identify Himself as the Messiah, the Son of God. Because Christ wants you to really know who He is, He went all-out to explain His true identity to you. He loves you so much.

On the contrary, Satan hates you. He is your enemy, and he goes to great extremes in order to conceal his true identity. He masks himself in a web of lies because he does not want you to know who he is. He is sneaky. He is covert. He is a thief. What's more, he will never tell you who *you* truly are. But Jesus will.

Every Thursday, we will be looking at the "I AM" statements of Christ.

These are seven sayings of Christ that are found in the New Testament book of John. Interestingly enough, I find these sayings are in perfect sync with our study on *Ruth*. Knowing who Christ is helps us know who we are. My prayer for you is this (write your name in the space below):

Heavenly Father,
By the end of this study, may ___________________ have developed an accurate picture of Christ—
one she can hang on to, frame, and settle prominently on the dresser of her life! In Jesus' Name, Amen.

JOURNALING

- Do you have a favorite snapshot? What is it, who is in it, and where do you keep it?

  ____

  ____

  ____

- Jesus used words to give us a picture of Him. If you were to describe yourself to someone you had never met, what would you say?

  ____

  ____

  ____

- Steve Sawyer said, "Jesus is alive and well today." Do you believe that? How do you know it's true?

  ____

In Isaiah 53:2, what did the prophet Isaiah record as a physical description of Christ?

____

____

____

Considering there is one half of one verse on Christ's physical appearance, and loads more verses on His actual character and personality, why do you think people place such a great emphasis what Jesus looked like? Why do people want to know?

____

____

____

Turn to page 153 and pray for the *Orpah* you know today.

REALITY CHECK WITH DANYA

ME

So now that we've been in another world and swept away by it all, the curtain has dropped, the lights have come back on, and we have to return to the real world.

When I've been in a movie theater and then gone back outside into the light, I've had to squint and shade my eyes with my hand because the real world is a lot *harsher* than fantasy. The amazing thing about the story of Ruth is that it is not fantasy, it's real! And it is just as harsh as real life. There's real pain in this story. There are real problems and real people, and there's a real solution.

Just like in life when our pain and problems seem too real and too much to handle, there is a real solution. We're going to be discovering that solution, that answer, in this study—because the only right answer is JESUS!

My name is Danya Powell. I'm fifteen, and I'm going to be writing the *Reality Check* every Friday. I have two little brothers: David and Derek, and I've been homeschooled my whole life.

I started playing the piano when I was six and started teaching myself to play the guitar when I was twelve. I love music! I express myself through playing and writing songs. I've had amazing worship experiences alone in my room, just playing worship songs on the guitar or writing my own praises to God.

I also play basketball, and I have the most amazing team in the world! Being on a team has taught me a lot, as you'll see later on in this study. I've learned about how important it is to have good friends. I've learned that to respect is better than to reject. (You can't play like a team if you don't like and respect each other.) I've learned not to judge people. I've learned that doing the wrong thing has consequences.

> *I've learned not to judge people. I've learned that doing the wrong thing has consequences.*

I became a Christian when I was five. I can't remember a time in my life when I didn't know Jesus' love and what He did for me. I joined my youth worship band when I was eleven, and my dream is to one day be a contemporary Christian music artist. My goal is to serve God in everything I do. There have been times when I've strayed away, but I have come back. I am so grateful to God that He gladly takes me back! Everyday, I try to have time with God when I'm studying my Bible and talking with Him. I have discovered so much! I've found when I truly pray and ask God to make His word my craving, He does! I have gotten closer to God just by having a quiet time with Him for ten to twenty minutes a day.

My prayer for you is that God will touch your heart through this study and you will be able to feel His unconditional love raining down on you. I pray that you would be unashamed of the Gospel of Jesus Christ!

It's time to get real.

JOURNALING

- Take time to complete any unanswered questions and finish up any reading you need to do for Week One.

- Do some soul-searching about what God is teaching you. What is going on in your life, at home and with your friends?

____

____

____

- How can you apply the lessons you are learning?

____

____

____

- Are you praying Jennie's prayer? How are you seeing God answer it?

____

____

____

- Work on the Scripture passage you chose to memorize.

- Turn to page 154 and pray for your *Boaz*.

COMING UP NEXT

Dim the Lights

Monday
FAMILY MATTERS
>Naomi Heads for Home

Tuesday
LAND OF THE LOST
>Knowing where You're Going

Wednesday
GETTING PERSONAL
>Fan or Follower?

Thursday
PICTURE THIS
>I AM the Bread of Life—You are Satisfied

Friday
TAKE TWO
>Reality Check with Danya: Defined

FAMILY MATTERS

Read the Script
Ruth 1:6-13

NAOMI HEADS FOR HOME

Good news! The famine in Bethlehem is over!

As soon as Naomi got this information, she made plans to return—to go home. Ruth and Orpah packed their things and began the journey with her. But shortly after they set out, Naomi realized something: What was best for her, which would be to go back home to Bethlehem, may not be best for her daughters-in-law.

"Wait a minute, now, you two," she said pointedly. "You are not going with me. You need to go back to Moab, to your own mothers and to your homes." Please don't miss the tenderness shown in this gracious rebuke. Naomi loved these girls. They shared a common bond in their love for Mahlon and Kilion. They were forever bound by the boys' lives, and they would be forever bound by their deaths. They were family—a broken, beaten, devastated family—but still, a family.

Naomi's wish for her daughters-in-law was that they would find rest, meaning security, in the home of another husband. In that ancient time and place, marriage was vitally necessary to a woman's existence. Without a man to provide a source of revenue and a place of protection, a woman was left on her own to make whatever meager way she could. Naomi wanted her daughters-in-law to enjoy the security of marriage, not the miserable, barely-getting-by life of widowhood.

Israelite law accommodated for the tragedy of widowhood. If a man died before he fathered any sons, the Jewish law gave the right of redeeming the property and possessions of the dead man to the closest relative (usually a brother), who was called a *goel*. In English, we use the phrase, "kinsman redeemer" to best express the role this person played. By the custom of the day, the *goel* was also responsible for marrying the widow, and the first son born through their union would be the heir of the widow's first husband. I know it sounds unusual, but the law was in place to give the widow the liberty of a secure future and to give the dead man's family the peace of knowing his name, resources, and land would be passed on to the next generation.

The grieving Naomi had no hope because she saw no redeemer in her future.

In Naomi's family, there were no more sons. Mahlon and Kilion had no brothers for Ruth and Orpah to marry. In what might have been said rather sarcastically, Naomi called attention to the fact that she was not a candidate for conceiving more sons. At this point, she was probably thinking of how hopeless her life was. She did not want to drag the girls down into her wretched existence. She wanted them to stay in Moab, where they might have a chance at re-marrying by going back to their parents' homes and starting over. She did not envision Bethlehem offering any opportunities for second marriages to these two young Moabite women. She would not allow them to follow her.

The grieving Naomi had no hope because she saw no redeemer in her future. When she lost her husband and sons, she lost her own life, as well. Things would never be as they were. She was broken, beaten, and devastated by her condition. Look closely at Naomi. She is a picture of a world that is broken, beaten, and devastated by its sinful condition. Now look even more closely at yourself.

Without Christ, you are broken, beaten, and devastated by the weight of your sins.

Without Christ, you have no hope.

Without Christ, you have no future.

However, there is good news! You don't have to settle for a meager existence. You don't have to live a life of famine! There is a Redeemer who brings hope to your present sinful condition today. Right now.

This week, we will be discussing the dark journey back to Bethlehem. It is illuminated only by the light of our living Redeemer who waits to satisfy us at the house of bread.

JOURNALING

- Read Jeremiah 29:10-14. Copy verse 11 here.

____

____

____

- How does God encourage us to seek Him? (Jeremiah 29:13)

____

____

____

- Why do you think Naomi is heading home? What do you think she expects to find there?

Write about the world around you. How is it broken by sin? How can you tell the hurting people you know about the Redeemer, Jesus?

Turn to page 150 and pray for the *Mahlon* you know today.

NOW PLAYING: LAND OF THE LOST

Read the Script

Ruth 1:6-13 (Read it again!) and Luke 24:13-35

KNOWING WHERE YOU'RE GOING

Waaaaay back in 1975 there was a popular song that rocketed to the top of the charts, inviting people to ponder some weighty questions: *Do you know where you're going to? Do you like the things that life is showing you? Where are you going to? Do you know?*

In the passage you re-read today, Naomi, Ruth, and Orpah were headed for Bethlehem. In the additional passage, a man named Cleopas was traveling with a friend down the road to Emmaus, centuries after the time of Ruth and just a few days after the crucifixion of Jesus Christ. It is another journey traveled by people who were greatly disillusioned by their circumstances. Cleopas and his friend were doing their best to cope with what appeared to be a hopeless situation. They were talking things over as they walked, and Jesus came and walked along with them. Strangely, they were kept from recognizing Him.[8] Usually I get stuck in this passage wondering why they did not recognize Jesus. I still do not know for certain. Perhaps if they had known Him immediately, they would not have listened to His lengthy and patient explanation of the events of the past couple of days. They would have missed out on the complete understanding He had come to give them.

As Cleopas and his friend backtracked over every detail of Christ's death, they could not wrap their heads around the apparent reality they tried to face: The Lord was dead, and so were their dreams for Israel's redemption. But there was Jesus, right there with them! They didn't know it, but He was walking with them and listening to them. Their grief, like Naomi's, was nearly unbearable. They could hardly process their pain. Their hope was crucified with Jesus.

--- ★ ---

The Lord was dead, and so were their dreams for Israel's redemption.

--- ★ ---

Have you ever felt like your hope has died?

Have you looked at situations in your life and seen your hope fall, a victim of circumstance?

How did the risen Christ resurrect the hope of Cleopas and his friend? He began to give them God's Word. He explained the stories of Moses and all the prophecies concerning the Messiah.[9] As the God-Man Jesus, He had tried many times to tell His followers that He would have to die. Here, as the Resurrected Son, He interpreted the Scripture along with the current events and showed them how the puzzle fit together. The same goes for us. We are not going to understand the significance of our own current events—the goings-on of our world as well as the daily activities of our individual lives—without God's Word and His Spirit coming alongside us to offer wisdom and peace.

Do you get what you're hoping for? When you look behind you there's no open door? What are you hoping for? Do you know? Decades ago Diana Ross sang this song, and today the questions are still good ones. We live in the land of the lost, but generation after generation is hard-wired by God to hope, dream, and expect. What were Cleopas and his friend hoping for? A wealthy, warrior King? The Jews' long-awaited Messiah did not come as expected. Losing hope, they were disappointed and disheartened. I've been there, and so have you. Can you identify with Naomi, who was dealing with the death of a loved one? Or do you connect with Mahlon and Kilion, who may have suffered from lifelong health problems? Perhaps, like Jesus, you have had to deal with a friend's betrayal.[10] Day after day God allows what we do not expect, what we did not ask for, and what we do not understand to happen along life's journey.

If you are on the road to Emmaus, unsure of who Christ is and struggling with the current events of your personal life, Jesus is waiting to reveal Himself to you through His Word. He longs to bring your hope back to life and to guide you to a powerful, purposeful walk with Him.

JOURNALING

Many times God uses the pain in our lives to draw us to a relationship with Him. When Cleopas and his friend invited Christ to share a meal with them, they were accepting His friendship and offering Him theirs. It is then, as Christ began to break the bread and serve them, their eyes were opened and they recognized Him. What about you? Would you like a relationship with Christ? If you know Him, would you like to know Him even better? Invite the Lord to reveal Himself to you in a deeper way today. Spend time writing down a prayer to Him now. Give Him your current events, and put your hope in Him alone.

____

____

____

____

____

Turn to page 151 and pray for the *Naomi* you know today.

GETTING PERSONAL

Read the Script
Ruth 1:14-18

FAN OR FOLLOWER?

I knew something was wrong when I knelt down to pray that night. I hadn't even gotten any words out. It was simply the act of kneeling and bowing that startled me into realizing, for the first time in my life, the familiar posture felt suddenly foreign. It had been a long time, I must admit, since I had prayed. But still, I knew prayer was not supposed to feel so empty.

It was the summer before my senior year of high school. I had spent those carefree days of vacation with the wrong attitude, at the wrong places, and in the company of the wrong people. On that particular night, I was in my bedroom, listening to the radio and thinking about how cool it was that I was going to be a senior. That caused me to take an objective look at how I spent the previous three years of high school. What had I accomplished? As a student, I had done all right. But what about as a person? The Lord brought to my mind the faces of a couple of Christian girls at school. They had a far better witness than mine. These young women stood out because they were more than just "good kids." I would always remember them as Christ followers.

I had spent a lot of my time just being angry. I couldn't stand many of the people I went to school with. They had teased me relentlessly in middle school and completely ignored me in high school, and I was mad. I couldn't forget, and I wouldn't forgive. I could give up the idea of anyone thinking of Christ and me in the same sentence. It occurred to me that for the most part, my high school years had been wasted, squandered by the lukewarm testimony of an immature Christian. That night, when I bowed my head, it was like nobody was there. I didn't know what to say or do. Feelings of remorse and regret began to fill my soul. Only one word came tumbling over my lips: *Father!* And then everything changed.

--★--

...my high school years had been wasted, squandered by the lukewarm testimony of an immature Christian.

--★--

His presence filled my little room as I asked Him to forgive me. The wall of unconfessed sin I had built over the course of time collapsed as He proved His faithfulness and forgave me, true to His Word. I repented that night and my life took on a new direction as I began to truly follow Christ.

There would be other times in my life when I would stumble and fall and find myself in the wrong place at the wrong time with the wrong people. But my focus, my goal, and my heart's desire was (and still is) to be His, completely His and completely surrendered to His will for my life.

The two verses you read today are full of meaning. Naomi, Ruth, and Orpah have come to a crossroads, a place where a decision has to be made: Bethlehem or Moab? Ruth chose Bethlehem. Orpah chose Moab.

Going back to Moab meant that Orpah was choosing to return to a land of many gods. She was giving up Jehovah, the one true God! But had she ever truly made a decision to follow Him? As the wife of a Hebrew man, she was introduced to Jehovah God, and she may have truly admired Him, but there is a big difference between being a fan and a follower. When Jesus walked around in the flesh on Planet Earth, He did not offer people membership in His fan club. He wasn't looking for fans! He doesn't want to be simply admired. He wants to be followed. Worshiped. Adored. He wants you to give your life away.

Ruth gave up her home, her family, and all that was familiar to her to follow the grieving Naomi to a land she had never seen and a people she had never known, all for a God who had become so real to her that she knew she could trust Him completely. She gave her life away in order to keep in close pursuit of the only God she had found worth following.

JOURNALING

Are you a Jesus fan? Do you wear the t-shirts and the bracelets but fall short when it comes to actually being a Jesus follower?

____

____

On a scale of 1 to 10, 10 being the best, rate your prayer life. How long has it been since you prayed?

____

____

Do you need to forgive someone? Your relationship with God is damaged when there is unforgiveness in your life. Ask God to show you if there is.

____

____

____

🎬 Is there unconfessed sin in your life? What steps will you take to be completely surrendered to Christ?

____

____

____

🎬 Turn to page 152 and pray for the *Ruth* you know today.

I AM THE BREAD OF LIFE

Read the Script
John 6:27-35

YOU ARE SATISFIED

Why do people seek Christ? What prompts a person to go looking for Him? In the passage you read today, the people were motivated by the incredible signs that were a daily part of Christ's ministry. They wanted to witness the wonders and get full on the feelings that followed the Anointed One. They didn't really want to know Him. They were along for the ride. If the ride started to get bumpy, they would be the first to get off.

When Tia came to my church a few months ago, she was looking for a way out. She was unemployed, a drug addict with a criminal record. She knew she needed to make some changes in her life. She had tried before and failed miserably. There was something about our church, however, that seemed to draw her in. She came a few times for services. Then one Sunday, she spoke to our pastor. He asked me if I would be a friend and mentor to Tia. "Of course," I replied quickly—maybe too quickly.

A few minutes later, I realized a relationship with Tia was way out of my comfort zone! How in the world would we ever connect? I had never used drugs, never been arrested, never even gotten a parking ticket. As I looked into Tia's eyes, I saw emptiness. It was like looking in a dark closet. I made plans to meet with her the following Wednesday evening at five o'clock.

I began praying for Tia immediately, and asking God where I should start in the mentoring process. I hate admitting this, but I was half-hearted about the whole thing. *Why get in an uproar?* I thought. *We serve the Lord in an inner city church. Over the years, lots of people have dropped in only to drop out. She probably won't even show up Wednesday.*

But she did.

The Lord met with us that evening as she shared her life with me. Her addiction had cost her a marriage and two sons, who lived with their dad. Drugs had caused numerous health problems and bought her a criminal record, which affected employment opportunities.

"So why do you take drugs?" I asked.

She smiled and answered simply, "For the feeling it gives me."

--- ★ ---

As I looked into Tia's eyes, I saw emptiness.

--- ★ ---

"What kind of feeling is worth this destruction?" I pressed. "Be specific."

Tia shrugged her shoulders. "I don't know exactly," she said. "Just good."

"But Tia," I challenged, "the feeling is temporary! When the feeling is over, your problems are still there."

I find it interesting that Jesus was dealing with much the same mindset from the crowd at Capernaum. They sought Him for a short-term solution to their hunger. They wanted Him for the healing He could give to a temporary body, a body that would eventually die. When Jesus declared, "I am the bread of life," he was explaining to the people through this visual image that just as bread was necessary in order to survive physically, accepting Him as their Messiah was essential if they wanted to survive spiritually. Our spirits are eternal. They will never die. Unlike a body that depreciates and a stomach that is never full, Jesus provides a way for our spirits, our souls, to be completely satisfied.

Jesus Christ is the bread of life. He is food for our souls. A Jewish audience could quickly relate to bread. It was a staple of their diet. Today, despite the varied diets people subscribe to that avoid bread altogether, it remains a global reference point. All people need bread. We all need sustenance to live.

Picture this: At Christ's birth, He was laid in a manger—a feeding trough—and God showed in this amazing detail the Christ child as the bread in Bethlehem. Without Him, we will experience spiritual famine in our lives. We will be hungry for something, anything, and we will feed ourselves with what the world has to offer if we don't go to Christ first to fill our spiritual tummies. He alone can sustain you each and every day. Satisfaction guaranteed.

JOURNALING

- Do you look for short-term solutions to problems? What happens when something is "fixed" temporarily?

____

____

____

____

- Do you think people look at Jesus as a temporary fix? Do you know people who look to him to fix their current situation, but they are not willing to hand over their lives to Him? Explain.

____

Are you looking to Christ to fill all the empty spaces in your life? Think about it. Where do you go when you feel empty, bored, or cranky? Where do you go when you feel lonely, rejected, or hurt?

Ask God to show you anywhere you might be putting something before Him, whether it's people, food, video games, or a hobby that has become a compulsion. Pray that He will lead you to seek your satisfaction in Him. Record your prayer here.

Turn to page 153 and pray for the *Orpah* you know today.

REALITY CHECK WITH DANYA

DEFINED

I sat in an old church van thinking about all the things that had happened that night. Our church mission team was in Benton, TN, and we were coming back from a Backyard Bible School we were helping run. I was away from home, away from my friends, and away from the Internet!!! All the youth that had planned on going had backed out. And to top it all off, I had woken up the morning of the mission trip with a swollen tongue from an allergic reaction to gum, of all things! I couldn't eat or talk or sing without pain, and I was responsible for leading the music for the Bible School!

Looking back on it now, I can see that God really wanted to get my attention. During the ride there and for most of the first day, I couldn't talk, which meant I had a lot of time to listen. I was in prayer for most of the time, and I had many other people praying for me, too. But that first night, it was still swollen, and it still hurt. I couldn't even eat breakfast! Sometimes, though, God works at the eleventh hour. Around an hour before I was supposed to start the music, the swelling went down completely! I could talk and sing!

In the van, I started thinking about the miracle that had just taken place. God really was there for me, and He really did come through for me! I thought about how a few months before, I had started falling away from God, and I really wasn't being the person that I needed to be. I was trying to define myself the way the world does.

Who was I going to be?

Was I going to wear all black?

Was I going to go for the designer clothes?

Was I going to be eclectic, where nothing matches, but it still goes together?

I was trying to define myself the way the world does.

Why couldn't I just be everything?

Who was I?

What group did I fit into?

I had really gotten into the world's way of thinking. But I felt empty. Sitting in that van, after teaching those kids about God and being in

His will, I was satisfied because I had discovered my definition: I am HIS. He is the Bread of Life; I am satisfied.

1 Peter 2:9-10 says, "But you are a chosen people, a royal priesthood, a holy nation, a people belonging to God, that you may declare the praises of Him who called you out of darkness into His wonderful light. Once you were not a people, but now you are the people of God; once you had not received mercy, but now you have received mercy."

I would encourage you to memorize 1 Peter 2:9-10 and hide that promise of God in your heart. We fall away from God like the Israelites did. We make foolish decisions. We're not perfect. The beauty of this is that God is perfect. Let Jesus be your Bread. You will be satisfied. Let Jesus be your Life. You will be defined.

JOURNALING

- Take time to complete any unanswered questions and finish up any reading you need to do for Week Two.

- Do some soul-searching about what God is teaching you. What is going on in your life, at home and with your friends?

____

____

____

____

- How can you apply the lessons you are learning?

____

____

____

- Are you praying Jennie's prayer? How are you seeing God answer it?

____

____

- Work on the Scripture passage you chose to memorize.

- Turn to page 154 and pray for your *Boaz*.

COMING UP NEXT

BREAK A LEG

Monday
GIRLFRIENDS
>FEELINGS, FRIENDS, AND FOES

Tuesday
THE PRODIGAL
>LIVING WITH "IF ONLY'S"

Wednesday
A DIFFERENT WORLD
>FROM RICHES TO RAGS

Thursday
PICTURE THIS
>I AM THE LIGHT OF THE WORLD—YOU ARE NO LONGER IN DARKNESS

Friday
TAKE TWO
>REALITY CHECK WITH DANYA: REMEMBER

GIRLFRIENDS

Read the Script
Ruth 1:19-21

FEELINGS, FRIENDS, AND FOES

Can you imagine the trip back to Bethlehem? It would have been at least 60 miles, taking Ruth and Naomi about a week. Don't you think every step of the way reminded Naomi of the last time she traveled that road?

Then, she was headed in the opposite direction.

Then, she had a husband and two sons.

Then, she was Naomi, the pleasant one—going to a better life, dodging the famine of her homeland. Now, as she returned to Bethlehem, her life had changed direction along with her steps. Empty but for her sorrow, she arrived home with nothing. Do you think Naomi dreaded facing her friends? Do you think she wondered what they would think of her? Did she hasten her steps as she and Ruth got closer to the city? Or did she slow them down?

The women of the town were astonished when they saw how Naomi had changed. They almost did not recognize her. "Can this be Naomi?" they asked each other. Was this the Naomi they knew—the life-of-the-party, got-it-all-together Naomi—this wisp of a woman they saw coming into the city? Battered by grief, broken by sorrow, and abandoned by her husband and sons' deaths, Naomi had lost the twinkle in her eye and the tempo in her step.

A decade before, these women watched jealously as Naomi left the famine-stricken village with her prosperous family. What did the women think when they saw her return, traipsing back just as the first crop in years was ready to harvest? These Bethlehem women had toughed it out. They stayed behind because they had nowhere else to go. Did they glory in Naomi's return, her fall from high-society wife to destitute widow? Or were they moved to compassion upon seeing her?

While I would really like to tell you I would have been the kind of person to welcome Naomi with open arms, I've got to be honest. God has a way of showing us our true colors, and because of something that happened to me recently, I don't have to speculate. I know exactly what my first reaction would have been.

-- ★ --

Empty but for her sorrow, she arrived home with nothing.

-- ★ --

You see, recently I was talking with a friend I had not seen in years. We went to high school together. She still lives in the town where we grew up, and she was catching me up on several old friends. Then she mentioned that she had seen one girl in particular—one of those "mean girls" I had struggled to forgive—and this girl had gained a lot of weight. I am ashamed to admit I could not suppress a smile at this information, and a thrill of pleasure ran through my wicked flesh at the news. I had to repent before God because those feelings were wrong. I realized I had not totally forgiven this girl. If I had, I would not have been rejoicing in her difficulties.

Girlfriends. Good grief.

Girls don't forget. Nope, we remember long and hard. We commit to memory every feeling, friend, and foe. Our mental records are well-documented, and our emotional search engines perform at optimum speed, retrieving trivial information at the mere mention of a name. This can be both good and bad. It's great to remember the kindnesses shown to you and to be thankful for good times and close friends. But remembering hurts makes it hard to forgive. We females can have a sickening bent for revenge. At the same time, we girls can pull together and accomplish great feats of love. Girlfriends become especially important during your teen years. This, too, can be both good and bad. God can use your friends to call you to a closer walk with Him. The enemy, however, can use your friends to distract you and tear your focus away from Christ.

I think after the initial shock wore off, after the surprise of seeing just how the flight to Moab had turned out for Naomi, these women were moved to mercy. They rushed to greet her, calling her by name. "Naomi! Pleasant One!" they must have exclaimed warmly. "Welcome home!"

Naomi, however, did not want to be known as *Pleasant One* anymore. She asked to be called *Mara*, which means "bitter." Her life had changed so drastically she felt her name should be changed, too. She was no longer the pleasant one they remembered. She was bitter. Throughout the book of Ruth, however, no one ever calls Naomi, "Mara." None of the women went along with this request. They met her at the city gate. They opened their arms in loving welcome, but they refused to attend her pity party. This proved their worth as true friends. They would not let her dwell on her bitterness. Instead, they would rally around her as she re-established her life in the house of bread.

JOURNALING

Ask yourself these three questions about your current friendships:

1. Does this person encourage me in my walk with Christ?

2. Can I trust this person to give me godly advice when I have a problem?

3. Will this person be loyal to me through hard times as well as good times?

Look over these questions again. This time, ask yourself if you are the kind of friend you are looking for. Do you encourage your friends with kind words and a positive attitude? Are you faithful to support them in their Christian walk? Are you loyal?

____

____

____

____

____

____

Read Matthew 5:44. What does this verse tell you to do about the "mean girls" in your life?

____

____

____

Look up Ephesians 4:29. How can obeying this command lead to better friendships?

____

____

____

Find James 2:1. How might you miss out on some great friendships?

____

____

____

Turn to page 150 and pray for the *Mahlon* you know today.

NOW PLAYING: THE PRODIGAL

Read the Script
Ruth 1:22, Luke 15:11-24

LIVING WITH "IF ONLY'S"

It took a great deal of courage for Naomi to go back home. There are many times when people want to return to a home, or even a job or a friendship, and their pride prevents them from doing it. This can be especially hard for teens. Acknowledging you need a "do over" means owning the fact that you messed up.

Jesus told the story of the prodigal son, a young man who wanted to go home again. This impulsive young man wanted what the world had to offer. It looked good to him, so much better than life at home. He was not content with what God had given him. In fact, he had a severe case of what I call the "If Only's."

If only I didn't have to live at home!

If only I could have my inheritance money to spend now!

If only I had different friends!

If only I could do what I want to do!

His father allowed him to have his "if only's." He gave his son his inheritance money early, and the young man took off, eager to experience "real life." In no time, the money was wasted. He was penniless. When his cash flow disappeared, so did his new "friends." The country that had promised so much was all smoke and mirrors when it entered a season of famine. This young man—the son of a wealthy landowner, the kid who had it all—soon found he was working for someone else, feeding pigs.

--★--

The country that had promised so much was all smoke and mirrors when it entered a season of famine.

--★--

Slopping around in the pigpen caused something to jolt this guy's memory, and he thought of home. Did he see his hands, calloused and grimy, and remember they were once the well-manicured, unblemished hands of a gentleman?

Was it the odor of the pigpen? Pigs were considered unclean according to Jewish law. Perhaps the sight and scent of this detested animal unnerved the boy.

Maybe it was the gnawing emptiness of a stomach ignored that was a new sensation to the well-fed son of the master. *"That brought him to his senses. He said, 'All those farmhands working for my father sit down to three meals a day, and here I am starving to death. I'm going back to my father.'"*[11]

Sometimes we get so far away from home—or from where we need to be—we forget exactly what it looked like or how it felt. We become so distracted by our current circumstances that it clogs our memory's hard drive. However, if something is allowed to penetrate that obstruction, a flood of sights, sounds, and scents comes pouring down. I imagine that Naomi heard there was bread in Bethlehem, and she found herself suddenly drenched in a downpour of forgotten memories: *The scenes of childhood. The sounds of a family. The faces of old friends. The fragrance of a sacrifice to the Lord. The feeling of oneness among God's chosen people.* She came to her senses. She realized she didn't have to stay in Moab. She could go home.

Naomi never intended to return to Bethlehem empty-handed and broken-hearted. Yet she knew God had allowed life to happen as it did. Like Naomi, we can choose to go along with God's plan and rest in it, or we can choose to be angry about how life has gone for us. Strangely enough, when bad things start happening, it can actually be a comfort to rest in the fact that God knows what is going on. He promises to be with us through the pain. He will never leave us! In fact, He is waiting for us to turn to Him in our crisis, and let Him fill those empty, hurting places life has left raw and bleeding. He wants us to see the big picture.

Despite Naomi's cries of emptiness, the author of Ruth skillfully invites the reader to see God's big picture. For one thing, it was the end of the famine. It was the beginning of the barley harvest. All of Bethlehem considered this a time of hope! And if you will take a closer look, you will see that Naomi was not completely empty nor truly alone. She came back home with her faith in her heart and a friend by her side.

JOURNALING

- Write down a definition of "humble" used as a verb and as an adjective.

____

____

____

____

____

____

- Have you ever been "humbled" by a situation? What happened? What did you learn?

Get Real!

____

____

____

____

____

- Do you know a person you consider to be humble? Why?

____

____

____

- How does the sin of pride affect your life? Do you own up to your mistakes?

____

____

____

- Copy James 4:10 in the space below.

____

____

____

- Turn to page 151 and pray for the *Naomi* you know today.

A Different World

Read the Script
Ruth 2:1-2

From Riches to Rags

Suzy Chandler* had the life every teenage girl in her high school wanted.

Her dad's successful business meant Suzy never had to want for anything. She had a shiny new sports car, a huge house, a swimming pool, and a closet crammed full of clothes and shoes. Her friends were the popular crowd, and Suzy was always right in the thick of things. Her bubbly personality made her sparkle from head to toe, and you knew if you were around her for any length of time, you were going to have fun. She would make sure of it!

When Suzy left home to attend a small private college, she had no reason to think anything would change. She planned to pursue a degree in business and eventually take over her father's company. Yet in a matter of twenty-four hours, Suzy found herself living in a different world.

The Dean of Women was waiting at the door of Suzy's first class with an icy smile. "I need to see you," she said. She explained that Suzy's check for tuition had bounced. When the faculty had investigated, they discovered that Suzy's bank account had been closed. Calls to her parents were not being returned.

Confused, Suzy quickly assured the dean there must be some mistake. When she called home, her mother answered and began crying as she confessed to Suzy they were in trouble. Her father had declared bankruptcy. His successful business was in ruins, and the family was going to lose everything.

With the sound of her mother's quivering voice playing over and over in her mind, Suzy immediately packed up her things and headed home. During the six-hour trip, she had a great deal of time to think and pray. She had never experienced a crisis her dad's money could not fix. Now there was no money. As the car sped over the interstate, Suzy realized the material things she had enjoyed all her life meant nothing to her now. She would sell her car, her jewelry, and her name-brand clothes. None of it mattered. Four hundred miles later, Suzy arrived home, ready to do whatever was needed to help her family.

Life is a series of unexpected events. When hard times hit, people still have to eat. They have to survive somehow. The Mosaic Law allowed for the inevitable fact that tragedy would happen. The Jews were

Discipline means doing what you don't want to do, when you don't want to do it, with a good attitude.

commanded to leave the corners of their fields unharvested, so they would be available to be gleaned by the poor. Needy people of those days would have been widows, like Naomi and Ruth, along with orphans and foreigners. This was an ingenious system of welfare. Those who had plenty were commanded to share and be generous. Those in need were given the opportunity to work and be productive. This is where we see Ruth headed—out to the fields to glean. She aligned herself with the harvesters. She was willing to work to support Naomi and herself.

One of the themes we see continuing to resurface in the book of Ruth is that of a disciplined heart. Discipline means doing what you don't want to do, when you don't want to do it, with a good attitude. That is a tall order, but it is not impossible. Ruth did it. Thus far, she has left her home, her family, her customs, and her religion to follow God. Now, she has stepped away from her pride. Did Ruth want to go out to the fields? I doubt it. She would not know anybody. It would be hard labor and physically demanding. Also, the fields were dangerous. But Ruth needed to eat, as did Naomi. As a result, Ruth—Mahlon's wife, a woman of standing—was willing to humble herself and glean along with the working girls.

Your character shines when you do what you have to do even when you do not want to. That is a sign of real maturity. Let God use the difficult events of your life to exercise your faith and build a holy toughness of character in your soul.

JOURNALING

- Where does your life show the most evidence of a disciplined heart? (for example: in your schoolwork, sports, a hobby, a talent)

____

____

____

- Where does your life need a boost of discipline? (for example: in your speech, attitudes, prayer life, cultivating your gifts and talents)

____

____

____

- Turn to page 152 and pray for the *Ruth* you know today.

I AM THE LIGHT OF THE WORLD

Read the Script
John 8:1-12

YOU ARE NO LONGER IN DARKNESS

When I was a teenager, I had an interesting way of dealing with my very messy bedroom.

I kept my door shut. This way, I thought my mom wouldn't notice the slob fest on the other side. This method actually worked for weeks at a time. Often, by the time my mom noticed, my room was in such chaos I would need her help to get things back in order.

When Mom helped me clean my room, we took a beautiful, sunny day, pulled open the curtains, and let the daylight fall over the room to illuminate the job before us. Then we pulled the furniture away from the walls and cleaned the dusty baseboards. We vacuumed underneath everything, washed the windows, and cleaned the light fixtures. What I thought of as a sloppy room, daylight and Mom exposed as filthy, grimy, and generally nasty. "If you would clean it up as you go," my mom explained, "your room would never get like this."

In the same way, we can close the door on certain places in our lives and pretend we don't have to deal with them. We may have secret habits we refuse to give up, forgiveness we have never offered, or private pleasures that are simply not pleasing to God. When Satan tells you no one will find out about your secret sins, you must remember he is a liar. Someone will find out, and what's more important, God already knows.

Today you met a woman who was literally caught in the act of adultery. Her sin was hidden behind secrecy and costumed in the shadows of night. Someone found out, however, and the darkness and deceit of her sin were exposed. In the light of early morning, some Pharisees brought her to Jesus and tried to get Him to decide what legal action would be taken against her. It was a set-up. If Jesus said, "No problem. Let her go," they would claim He had no respect for the Law of Moses. But if Jesus ordered, "She should be put to death. Stone her," they would accuse Him of being inconsistent with the character of the Messiah He claimed to be—the one who welcomed prostitutes and tax collectors.

So how did Jesus respond to their tactics? He invited any of her accusers who were without sin to cast the first stone. One by one, the Light revealed their sin. The only one without sin was Jesus, and He was not going to throw any stones at all. He redeemed the woman's

--★--

When Satan tells you no one will find out about your secret sins, you must remember he is a liar.

--★--

---

life from the grave and handed it back to her with a simple command: "Go now and leave your life of sin."

The prophet Isaiah foretold the ministry of Christ this way, "The people walking in darkness have seen a great light. . ."[12] What does light do?

It gets rid of darkness.

It enables you to see things clearly.

It warms things up.

Once you begin to walk closely with Jesus, you will find His light will dispel the darkness and cause you to see things more clearly, from His viewpoint. Staying close to the Light will keep the Christian flame in your heart burning brightly for Him. The bright light of Christ, however, can be uncomfortable at times.

Picture this: Jesus is the Light. How close will you get to the Light that reveals even secret sins? As a college student, I experienced a rapid season of growth as a Christian. It took a while for my lifestyle habits to catch up with what I was learning in God's Word. A girl in my dorm (who knew I was a Christian) was constantly heckling me and belittling everything I did, from the clothes I wore to what I watched on TV in the lobby. I asked my friend Jennie how to deal with this girl. "People on this campus are looking for real Christians," she explained. "Talk is cheap. This gal is looking at your life! As you get closer to the Light, more dirt will be exposed. Clean it up as you go."

JOURNALING

- It is hard to live a life above reproach, yet that is what we are called to as Christians. Look up 1 Timothy 4:12 and write it here.

____

____

____

- How can you set an example for other believers in your speech?

____

____

____

____

In your love for people?

____

____

____

In your faith and devotion to God?

____

____

In your purity?

____

____

Has the Light uncovered any sins you need to talk to God about? Don't hesitate! He's waiting for you. Write your prayer here.

____

____

____

____

Turn to page 153 and pray for the *Orpah* you know today.

REALITY CHECK WITH DANYA

REMEMBER

When I was in the eighth grade, our junior varsity girls' basketball team was good. But we weren't great. When we lost, we got mad, especially if there was one girl on the other team we just couldn't stop. We were mad there was someone *better* than us.

There was one basketball game that season that, to us, was World War III. There was one girl on the other team we couldn't stop. We didn't like her. When one of our girls got a steal and was going for a lay-up, this girl jumped up to stop her and knocked her down. Our girl was out of the game with a hurt ankle! That did it.

The next time this girl had the ball, I came up behind her, and, well, she ended up on the floor. I felt just a little bad about it, but only because I got called for an intentional foul, she got to shoot free-throws, and they won. My actions were even justified when one of her own teammates said that she had deserved the foul!

I didn't give the incident a second thought, unless it was to laugh about it with my teammates, until practice the next season. We were playing for the varsity now, and our team spirit was growing.

A new girl walked in the gym.

She looked pretty cool. She and her mom watched us practice. The coach told us that she wanted to join the team. So, as soon as practice was over, I ran over to introduce myself and talk to her. Her name was Crystal, and she was a freshman. She looked really anxious, and her mom said she was dying to shoot. I grabbed the nearest ball I could find and motioned for her to go to the foul line. She did, and I started rebounding for her. There was something very familiar about her shooting form.

Girls don't forget. We remember long and hard.

Soon, some of the other girls joined us. We accepted Crystal immediately, and I was proud of that. Someone asked where she had gone to school before, and when she told us, there was dead silence. Then, we all lost it and started laughing. She looked at us like we were crazy. We remembered the school. And she remembered me, but she didn't know why. When she came in for practice the next week, I remembered exactly who she was.

Girls don't forget. We remember long and hard. We commit to memory every feeling, friend, and foe. Our team remembered Crystal.

We remembered how we felt when she knocked down our girl. I remembered knocking her down.

One night, I watched my DVD of that game. I watched and re-watched where our girl had gotten hurt. And Crystal hadn't knocked her down! Another girl had gotten in the way and tripped her. But we were looking at Crystal because we wanted to be mad at her. We wanted a reason to not like her. The next time I saw her, I apologized.

At the next practice, we also remembered how good she was. She was on our team now, and we accepted her. Now, when she gets knocked down, we're ready to help her up.

It's amazing how quickly feelings can change, isn't it?

Even though we don't talk about it a lot, our team learned something. Now, when we're in a game and we're getting mad at an opposing player, you'll hear someone say, "Don't get mad, she might be on our team next year."

Jesus accepted everyone. He loved everyone. He is the light for everyone. He's given us the amazing opportunity to show others His light and love by the way we live. Jesus has taken us out of the darkness, and He has given us His love. Shouldn't we show others the same love?

JOURNALING

- Take time to complete any unanswered questions and finish up any reading you need to do for Week Three.

- Do some soul-searching about what God is teaching you. What is going on in your life, at home and with your friends?

____

____

____

- How can you apply the lessons you are learning?

____

____

- Are you praying Jennie's prayer? How are you seeing God answer it?

____

- Work on the Scripture passage you chose to memorize.

- Turn to page 154 and pray for your *Boaz*.

COMING UP NEXT

BOY MEETS GIRL

Monday
STRANGE LUCK?
> GOD'S TIMING IS PERFECT

Tuesday
WHO'S THE BOSS?
> EVERYTHING AS UNTO THE LORD

Wednesday
THAT GIRL
> DEFINE BEAUTY

Thursday
PICTURE THIS
> I AM THE DOOR—YOU ARE SAFE INSIDE

Friday
TAKE TWO
> REALITY CHECK WITH DANYA: FOCUSED

STRANGE LUCK?

Read the Script
Ruth 2:3

GOD'S TIMING IS PERFECT

Did Ruth "just happen" upon Boaz's field? Was it a mere *coincidence* that she began gleaning in a field that belonged to a relative of her dead husband?

In order to answer those questions, think about these:

Is God's timing perfect?

Does He really order the steps of a righteous man, as His Word promises? Or do things happen randomly, and by some sort of strange luck just fall into place?

Once when I was traveling to speak at a parenting conference, I was chatting with the woman seated next to me on the plane. She was on her way to visit her sister, who just had her first baby. "Your sister needs a copy of my book for new moms!" I said enthusiastically. I always carry copies of *Baby Boot Camp* with me when I travel, so I scrambled around in my tote bag and pulled one out. "Would you like me to sign it for her?"

"Sure." My new friend smiled as she began flipping through the book. "But this one has already been signed."

What? I was so embarrassed. I quickly took a clean copy from my bag, signed it for her, and turned toward my husband Rich, seated on the other side of me. My cheeks were still flaming with embarrassment as he peeked in the book that had already been signed.

"Let's see," said Rich. "It says, *To Laura–God's timing is perfect!* Who is Laura?"

"I have no idea," I said, completely puzzled. "I don't even remember signing that book."

"Well, that's your handwriting," he stated.

"I guess it can be a prize for whoever we meet named 'Laura' at this conference," I laughed.

Once we arrived at the conference, I forgot about that pre-signed book. I was so busy speaking and meeting people that I wasn't even

Does He really order the steps of a righteous man, as His Word promises?

looking for anyone named Laura! Besides running my booth, Rich spent quite a bit of time talking with a young man who had a booth close to ours. He seemed troubled about something. On the last day of the conference, Rich brought the man over to meet me.

"Rebecca, this is Jack*," he said. "Jack and his wife have three little boys, and they just found out they are expecting again."

"How wonderful!" I exclaimed and picked up a book from my table. "Please take a copy of *Baby Boot Camp* home to your wife."

He smiled and took the book I offered. "She wanted to come with me this weekend," he said, "but she's not been feeling very well."

"Morning sickness?" I asked.

"Well, it's not just that," Rich interjected. "She's upset. Their families haven't been exactly enthusiastic about the news of the new baby."

Jack smiled ruefully as he explained. "Our boys are ages three, two, and six months. Our parents don't think we can manage a large family, and everything they have said so far has been hurtful and negative. My wife has been broken-hearted about their reaction."

"What's your wife's name?" I asked. "I'd like to pray for her."

"Her name is Laura."

Chills ran all over me as I reached for the book in his hands. "If her name is Laura, you've got the wrong book!" I went to my tote bag and pulled out the mysterious copy that had already been signed and set apart for Laura—a Laura that God knew would need it.

Jack, puzzled, took the book from me and read the inscription. "I don't understand," he began. Rich told him the story. He reached for his cell phone and called his wife. "Honey, you are not going to believe this." Then he proceeded to tell her the story! He read her the inscription in the book.

"Yes, honey," we heard him say. "That's what it says: *To Laura—God's timing is perfect!*"

After he hung up the phone, he said, "You may not believe this—"

"Oh, yes, we will," Rich assured him.

"Laura said she has been praying all weekend for God to give her a sign that He is in control. This book—this message with her name on it—this is it."

JOURNALING

- Do you believe in coincidences, or do you believe that God puts people, places, and events together? Look up Proverbs 16:9 and record it here.

____

____

____

____

____

■ Have you ever thought about God being interested in you in a personal way?

____

____

■ What are some ways God has spoken to you lately, through His Word, through your parents, or through a sermon or teaching you heard at church?

____

____

____

■ Do you long for the kind of relationship with God that is active and personal? Ask Him to help you grow closer to Him. That is the kind of prayer He loves to answer with a "Yes!" Write your prayer here.

____

____

____

____

____

____

■ Turn to page 150 and pray for the *Mahlon* you know today.

WHO'S THE BOSS?

Read the Script
Ruth 2:4, Ephesians 6:5-9

EVERYTHING AS UNTO THE LORD

One of my first jobs was working in a Christian bookstore.

My boss, Doug Hughes, was a godly man. You would not believe some of the things people said to him (such as, "I don't think you ought to be charging people for Bibles") and the fusses they made, but he handled everything with grace and dignity. Doug didn't raise his voice. He never let his customers or his employees cause him to become obviously annoyed or frustrated. I loved working for him. I did not know at the time what a rare treat it was to work for a Christian man like Doug, but I certainly found out in later years working for bosses who didn't follow Christ.

Despite how well I got along with Doug, there was one point on which we differed. Even though he sold all types of Christian music, he would only play worship music or Southern Gospel in the store. This was the mid 80's, when contemporary Christian music was finally coming of age. So many Christian artists were breaking out of the mold and sneaking into more popular genres of music, and I loved them all! But Doug believed that playing contemporary music would drive people out of the store rather than bring them in.

The first time Doug gave me the responsibility of closing, which meant working the evening hours by myself and then locking up, I popped a Steve Taylor tape into the store's sound system about sixty seconds after Doug had left. I admit today that Taylor's music was not something to shop by. It was new wave rock with edgy, in-your-face lyrics, and it sounded best when played at high volume. Doug did not allow me to play Taylor's music when he was there, but I reasoned I was in charge of the store, and I was going to do what I wanted. About 30 minutes later, Doug walked back in, having forgotten something. I was so busted!

I admit today that Taylor's music was not something to shop by.

I was ready to be reprimanded, even yelled at, but Doug remained unruffled. He smiled at me, went to the back room to retrieve the forgotten papers, said good night, and left again. I felt so bad. I replaced Steve Taylor with the kinder, gentler music Doug preferred, on a lower, more pleasant volume. We never spoke of that evening. In fact, as time went on, Doug gave me more responsibility in the store, and I worked harder than ever to please him and do things the way I knew he wanted them done.

In Ruth 2:4, Boaz's greeting to his employees was a typical Jewish greeting. It was spoken as frequently as today's catchphrase, "Have a nice day," is batted around. However, because God's chosen people knew the value and power of words, this greeting was never given in a light-hearted manner. It was never used as a joke. It was never said sarcastically. On this day, it was said as a prayer for the harvest workers, asking God for prosperity. Boaz's prayer encouraged his field hands in their work and let them know even in this task, God would join them.

The name Boaz, remember, means, "in him is strength." Bethlehem, as you recall, means, "house of bread." The Hebrew meaning of Jehovah is "the existing one." So if we take this verse and translate each name, it reads this way:

Just then *in him is strength* arrived from *the house of bread* and greeted the harvesters, "*The unchanging, eternal, self-existent God, the 'I am that I am,' a covenant-keeping God* be with you."[13]

"*The unchanging, eternal, self-existent God, the 'I am that I am,' a covenant-keeping God* bless you,"[14] they called back.

This is our first glimpse of Boaz. What do you see? I see a godly man.

We are not given a physical description of Boaz. In a future chapter, he will make reference to the fact that he is not young. In this passage, however, Boaz exhibited features most women would find quite attractive: his life-giving language and the respectful response he drew from those he employed. They were more than willing to work hard to please him and do things the way he wanted them done.

JOURNALING

- Referring to the Ephesians passage you read for today, explain how I was actually being disobedient *to God* by the way I acted when I was left in charge of the store.

____

____

____

- What are the qualities of a good boss?

____

____

____

- What are the qualities of a good employee?

How can you perform the job of *student* as unto the Lord?

Copy Ephesians 6:7 here.

Turn to page 151 and pray for the *Naomi* you know today.

THAT GIRL

Read the Script
Ruth 2:5-7, Psalm 139:1-18

DEFINE BEAUTY

Don't you love it? The boss noticed the working girl!

Boaz saw her when he was not looking for her, and strangely enough, Ruth garnered his attention without even knowing it. She managed to fascinate the most eligible bachelor in Bethlehem when romance was the last thing on her mind. How did that happen?

I want to be sure you get the real picture here. Ruth had been gleaning. When she caught the eye of Boaz, she did not look like a celebrity with makeup piled on and hair styled just so, inserted dramatically on a Hollywood set while the cameras rolled. No, you are reading an authentic scene from an actual account in God's Word. Our heroine was hot and sweaty. Her hands and feet were dirty. She smelled bad. Dressed in her working clothes, she looked no different from any other gleaner. But somehow, she stood out distinctly to Boaz. He noticed her immediately.

When Boaz asked his foreman about her, he was told she was the young Moabite woman, Naomi's daughter-in-law. The way the foreman referred to her indicates Boaz, like everyone else in town, was aware of the details. I wonder if Boaz suspected that the girl who had caught his attention was the girl he had already heard about, the one who left everything to follow the Existing One and to take care of her mother-in-law. Whatever the case, Ruth's reputation preceded her. Because Boaz knew her story, he saw more than a hard-working young woman that day. He saw Ruth's character, her good deeds, her devotion to God, and her compassion for another. He saw a beautiful woman.

What is beauty? In our culture, beauty is defined as physical perfection. But do you know what God, the Creator, has to say about physical beauty? Stop and dwell on the very essence of that question. What does God, the one who created us,

who designed our DNA,

who planned our personalities,

who chose our parents,

who knew we would sin,

--- ★ ---

She was everything I wasn't—perfect.

-- ★ --

and who sent a Savior just so He could be united with us for eternity—what does He have to say about physical beauty? He says it doesn't last.[15] It's temporary, fleeting.

To God, the one who made your face, your skin, and your hair, the things that are important have lasting significance and eternal value. In 1 Samuel 16:7, God explains that He doesn't make decisions or judgments the way people do. People judge by outward appearance, but the Lord looks at a person's thoughts and intentions—a person's heart.[16] True beauty comes from within.

When I was a girl, I had my own ideal of true beauty in actress/model Jaclyn Smith. She was everything I wasn't—perfect. Her white teeth glistened from glossy ads in magazines, where she flaunted her shiny hair and clear complexion and promised if I bought the right products, I would be perfect, too. It's easy for us females to get hung up on physical beauty and to pursue it, neglecting the makeover that needs to occur in our hearts. We all long to be the prettiest girl in the room. But if a girl is only pretty on the outside, she is as one-dimensional as a model in a print ad: flat, lifeless, and easily crumpled. Makeup can conceal blemishes and braces can straighten teeth, but the only way to have a beautiful heart is to invite the Master of the Makeover, Jesus Christ, to do a work on the inside, where it counts.

You see, God knows your story. He noticed you before you were ever born, and He loved you before you ever loved Him. His love does not balance on your appearance or your actions. It rests on the simple fact that He is the lover of your soul. You have managed to fascinate the Most High God without even knowing it! You were made for Him. That's what makes you a real beauty.

JOURNALING

What is your definition of beauty?

____

____

____

____

Would you consider yourself preoccupied with the pursuit of physical beauty?

____

____

____

How does knowing God's thoughts on true beauty change the way you see yourself?

____

____

____

____

Copy Psalm 139:14 in the space below. Do you believe you are fearfully and wonderfully made? Say this verse aloud. Believe what God tells you.

____

____

____

____

____

Turn to page 152 and pray for the *Ruth* you know today.

PICTURE THIS — I AM THE DOOR

Read the Script
John 10:1-10

YOU ARE SAFE INSIDE

As we pulled in the driveway, it seemed like any other Sunday night to me. My parents, however, knew something was different—wrong, in fact—because they had instantly noticed the door to our home was slightly ajar. My sister and I were instructed to wait in the car while Daddy and Momma went in the house. After what seemed like several minutes, my daddy came back out to the car. "Girls," he said, "the house has been robbed."

I had never seen such chaos in the home my mother always kept so neat and tidy. The thieves took drawers and dumped their contents on the floor as they rifled through our belongings looking for anything of worth. They ripped the mattresses off the beds searching for money. Even kitchen cabinets were opened and emptied as they hunted for cash, jewelry, and valuables.

It was my mother who noticed my glass piggy bank on my bed. "Will you look at that?" she said softly. One of the burglars had gone to the trouble of shaking the coins out of the thin slot on my bank. I was eight years old at the time, and I remember thinking, "It was nice of the robber not to break my piggy bank."

Today, I understand there was nothing "nice" about anything those burglars did that night. They were not thinking of my family or me or of anyone but themselves. As a child, I foolishly believed the thief had my best interest at heart when he chose not to break my bank. I wasn't looking at the devastation around me. My mother lost her jewelry, her silver, and for a while, her peace of mind. My dad lost his camera and his guitar. No, whoever shook my bank for small change did not have me in mind. It must have been more convenient to shake it than to break it and have to pick out the coins from among glass shards.

"Girls," he said, "the house has been robbed."

Satan is a thief, yet it is easy to become confused about our enemy when he comes cleverly disguised as "nice." Take a look at Judas, for example.

Judas, the disciple who betrayed Christ, lived with Jesus and His followers for several years. He was "nice" to all the disciples. They trusted him enough to make him their treasurer—the keeper of the money bag[17]. Even the way Judas betrayed the Master was "nice;" he betrayed Christ with a kiss. This is the perfect example of the enemy. He will live with you, share the table with you, and treat you as a friend. Nevertheless, he will betray you every time.[18]

Bible teacher Beth Moore once cautioned that we Christians would do well to beware the "Judas sins" that betray our Christian walk. These are sins, she explained, that try to be a friend and a comfort to you—sins that kiss you on the cheek. We may be walking in agreement with the enemy on these sins because they are so "nice" and feel so good. How about overeating? Gossip? Fighting with your siblings? Disrespecting your parents? Badmouthing those in authority? Allowing worldly influences access to your heart via television and the Internet? Neglecting Bible study and prayer because you don't have time? We are quickly surrounded by devastation when we call our enemy "nice."

Picture this: Jesus is the Door. You are safe inside. Choose to let Him decide what and who comes in and out of your life. He will protect you from the ravages of sin by staying shut tight against gossip and worldly influences. He will permit easy access to His love, allowing you to show grace to your sibs and honor to your parents. He will never break His promises to you. He is so much more than nice. He is the lover of your soul. Does that mean nothing bad or scary will ever happen to you? Well, it means whatever does happen to you has to go through Him first. Your steps are ordered by the Master who loves you for who you are! He has your best interest at heart.

JOURNALING

- In what way is Satan like a thief?

____

____

____

- Police officers and detectives dust for fingerprints in order to solve crimes. If you were to dust for Satan's fingerprints in your life, where would you find them?

____

____

____

- Are you in agreement with the enemy on any of your personal sins? Which ones?

____

____

____

🎬 Write John 10:10 in the space below.

____

____

____

____

🎬 Turn to page 153 and pray for the *Orpah* you know today.

REALITY CHECK WITH DANYA

FOCUSED

I loved our church. Lots of people went there, and about fifteen kids were in my grade alone! I had tons of friends, and it was a comfort to know they all believed what I believed. All of them came to church with their parents; everybody knew everybody. We dressed up nicely to come, and it was just great!

One day, close to my eleventh birthday, Daddy told my brothers and me that we might be going to a new church for a little while to help it minister to people. We were fine with that, except when the "little while" turned into "way longer than I wanted to be there." This new church wasn't like our old one. It was a big building, but not a lot of people went there. There were about 15 kids in the whole children's department! There were no girls my age, and I had to be in the same class with my little brother, which didn't work well with my big sister pride. Most of the kids came to church without their parents, and it was very awkward for me to come to church in a skirt when these kids came in jeans and T-shirts. I didn't like it.

Sometimes, God puts us where we don't want to be, when we don't want to be there, so we can be what He wants us to be. His timing is perfect; His plan is perfect, and He is trustworthy.

When we let Jesus become our Door, when we let Him take control of what comes in and what goes out, what situations we are put into and which ones we avoid, our lives become what they were meant to be. It might not be easy. It might not be fun. It might not look like anything good can come out of it. But sometimes, the bigger picture is hidden from us until it has taken place.

God was breaking my pride, and I was beginning to understand. I stepped up my game.

When I look back and see all the wonderful things God has done in my life, I want to serve Him that much more! I want to do exactly what He wants me to do, and I want to do it with a joyful heart. His love for me is so great, and He pours it down so freely, it makes me love Him more.

Around six months after we had been going to the new church, I graduated into the youth group. Life changed. I started seeing more of the big picture. These kids wanted Jesus, and when they discovered what it was like to be in a relationship with Him, they got up early on Sundays and came to church even though their parents didn't. They crammed in homework so they could get there on Wednesday nights.

God was breaking my pride, and I was beginning to understand. I stepped up my game. I began developing relationships with people. I started paying more attention to what was going on. I wanted to be there helping people. I wanted to do what Daddy had tried to explain to us that we needed to do.

Soon, I started playing keyboard for the youth band and helping lead worship. A few months later, our band started leading worship once a month for contemporary services at our church. Soon after I turned twelve, I got to go into a studio and record a demo with the band. When I was thirteen, I got to sing with the band for the first time, and after that I started singing as well as playing. When I was focused on God, His plan for my life came into play.

God had me where He wanted me to be, so I could do what He wanted me to do, so I could be who He wanted me to be.

Sometimes we don't want to let God put us in situations where we feel *uncomfortable*. But when we look back, we will realize that He knew.

He knew.

JOURNALING

- Take time to complete any unanswered questions and finish up any reading you need to do for Week Four.

- Do some soul-searching about what God is teaching you. What is going on in your life, at home and with your friends?

____

____

____

- How can you apply the lessons you are learning?

____

____

- Are you praying Jennie's prayer? How are you seeing God answer it?

____

____

- Work on the Scripture passage you chose to memorize.

- Turn to page 154 and pray for your *Boaz*.

COMING UP NEXT

AND NOW,
THE STAR OF THE SHOW

Monday
SAFE HARBOR

PROTECTING RUTH'S PURITY

Tuesday
LOVE CONNECTION

PREPARING RUTH'S WAY

Wednesday
STATE OF GRACE

PRESERVING RUTH'S DIGNITY

Thursday
PICTURE THIS

I AM THE GOOD SHEPHERD—YOU ARE CALLED BY NAME

Friday
TAKE TWO

REALITY CHECK WITH DANYA: UNASHAMED

SAFE HARBOR

Read the Script
Ruth 2:8-9

PROTECTING RUTH'S PURITY

Sometimes you need a protector.

When I was a freshman in high school, we had to take gym class for a mandatory physical education credit. My teacher, Coach Gotallday*, was never in a hurry to start class. Once we changed into our gym clothes, we had to form a line so he could take roll. We were usually left standing there for quite some time, with no supervision.

One guy in particular would go around grabbing us girls while we waited, lifting us up in all-consuming bear hugs. This young man was a super athlete and really cute, and several of the girls enjoyed his attention. However, I was uncomfortable with his hugs. I didn't want him anywhere near me, and when he realized I didn't want his attention, it became a big game to him. Every day he waited for me. Every day he would literally pick me up off the floor and squeeze me in a bone-crushing hug, pressing me as close as possible to himself. Coach Gotallday was never around, and since he was also known as Coach Gottawin, I knew he would never do anything in the way of disciplining one of his star athletes. I wasn't sure what to do about my situation.

If I told what was happening, how would I explain it? None of the other girls were complaining. As a 15-year-old girl who had battled her way through several years of the public school system, I had enough experience to know my school life would be even more miserable if I had to live with the peer consequences of getting one of the most popular boys in school in trouble. It looked as though I had nowhere to go. Then, by God's grace, I thought of Jake.

Jake Stewart* was a senior and one of the biggest guys on the football team. More importantly, Jake was a Christian. He loved the Lord. We had a class together and had gotten to be pretty good friends. One day, my problem came spilling out, and I told him what was happening in gym. I didn't know what to call it at the time, but I was experiencing the bullying effects of sexual harassment. With a quiet firmness, Jake said, "Don't worry. I'll take care of it." I don't know how he took care of it; I never asked him. All I know is I never had another problem in gym class.

> *It looked as though I had nowhere to go.*

Ruth willingly went to the gleaning fields, certainly aware of the dangers she faced as an unprotected, widowed woman in a man's world. "Sexual harassment" might be a relatively new term, but it is simply a fresh label for an ancient problem. The U. S. Equal Employment Opportunity Commission defines sexual harassment as unwelcome sexual advances, requests for sexual favors, and other verbal or physical conduct of a sexual nature that explicitly or implicitly affects an individual's employment, unreasonably interferes with an individual's work performance, or creates an intimidating, hostile, or offensive work environment.[19]

How could such a thing happen among God's chosen people? Why would there be such ungodly behavior in the Promised Land? Remember: The story of Ruth takes place in the days when the judges ruled. Bethlehem was no longer known for widespread godliness. It was commonplace for women to be endangered by molestation and rape on the job. But not in Boaz's field! He had instituted possibly the world's first sexual harassment policy. His fields were safe because he had warned the young men who worked for him not to bother the women.

Many years after high school, I was speaking at a women's retreat where I actually met Jake's mother. I learned firsthand what I had already known in my heart: Jake was the product of a godly mom. He had learned how to protect and respect women from her. Boaz, likewise, as we will see in tomorrow's lesson, learned to respect women from his mom. From her, he learned a godly man's responsibility toward protecting a girl's purity.

JOURNALING

Do you remember how Ruth managed to arrive at Boaz's fields to work? How did she come upon this "safe" place?

____

____

____

Have you ever been a victim of sexual harassment? What happened to make you feel threatened? What did you do about it? After you journal about the situation, please share the information with your mom or dad. I wish I had told my parents what was going on.

____

____

____

____

____

- Are the boys you know respecters of women?

  ____

  ____

- Are there events in your life where you have seen God acting as your protector?

  ____

  ____

  ____

  ____

- In verse 8, Boaz gives Ruth two instructions that will further help her to be safe. List them here.

  ____

  ____

  ____

  ____

- How do you know that God is looking out for your purity? How can you cooperate with Him?

  ____

  ____

  ____

  ____

- Turn to page 150 and pray for the *Mahlon* you know today.

LOVE CONNECTION

Read the Script
Ruth 2:10-14

PREPARING RUTH'S WAY

Here's the story,
of a lovely lady,
who was bringing up three very lovely girls.
All of them had hair of gold,
like their mother,
the youngest one in curls.
Here's the story,
of a man named Brady,
Who was busy with three boys of his own.
They were four men,
living all together, yet they were all alone.

Till the one day when the lady met this fellow. . .

Sound familiar?

Everybody loves to hear the story of how their parents met.

Boaz, I think, was no different. His parents must have shared a very special love story, the beginning of which is found in the second chapter of the Old Testament book of Joshua. You see, the godly man Boaz was the son of a prostitute. His mother was Rahab of Jericho.

In order for the Israelites to take possession of the Promised Land, they had to conquer it city by city. Under Joshua's leadership, two spies were sent into the city of Jericho to check it out before the Israelites attacked. Rahab the prostitute provided their lodging and helped them escape from city officials. In exchange, she asked them to spare her life and the lives of her family members. They agreed. Although Jericho was totally demolished, we are told the spies kept their end of the bargain.

Boaz, then, grew up hearing this fascinating story of how his parents met.

> *Joshua let Rahab the harlot live—Rahab and her father's household and everyone connected to her. She [at the time the book of Joshua was written] is still alive and well in Israel because she hid the agents whom Joshua sent to spy out Jericho.* [20]

Obviously Rahab and her family joined the Israelites and accepted Jehovah as their God. Sometime later Rahab married an Israelite, Salmon, (who could have been one of the spies, since the spies are never named) and gave birth to Boaz.

Boaz, then, grew up hearing this fascinating story of how his parents met. As he got older, his mother might have shared more of the details with him. For example, she might have shared with him how grateful she was to Israel—they spared her life and introduced her to Jehovah, whom she would forever claim as God. She may have also talked to him about how difficult it was to assimilate into the nation of Israel as a foreigner. Of course, Rahab could have been almost like a heroine to them, because she saved the lives of their two spies and was pivotal in God's hand as He gave Israel the great victory. I wonder, though, if the other Israelite women were always mindful of the fact that she had been a prostitute. I wonder how hard it was for her to make real friends among the people who had been her sworn enemies.

To Boaz, however, she was his beloved mom. All he had ever known of this woman was her devotion to Yahweh, the great I AM, and to her family. So why was Boaz being so nice to Ruth? Maybe she reminded him of his mom. Maybe he saw in Ruth the same heart for God that caused his mother, a prostitute, to sell out her country and lie to her king, all because she believed in the one, true God, and she was willing to lay down her life for Him.

Can you believe that God was preparing Boaz to accept this Moabite woman as his bride from the time he was a child? God had a plan—a plan that nothing would interrupt. Boaz grew up in the home of a woman who knew what it was like to be a foreigner among God's chosen people. He learned about money from a mom who was a shrewd business person and entrepreneur. He ate at the table of one who accepted others the way she had been accepted by God. He walked by the side of a person who had laid her life on the line for a God she had only heard about—a God she dared to believe was true. My goodness, Boaz must have been quite a man because he had quite a mom!

JOURNALING

- Boaz offers a prayer for Ruth, asking Jehovah Elohim to reward her for seeking her refuge under His wings. Look up Psalm 17:8, Psalm 36:7, and Psalm 63:7. Choose one of these verses to write in the space below.

____

____

____

____

____

List some of the ways God prepared Boaz to be attracted to Ruth.

____

____

____

____

____

Read Appendix B, "You're Israelites, Aren't You?" by Dr. Ralph F. Wilson.

Turn to page 151 and pray for the *Naomi* you know today.

MISSION: HIMpossible

Read the Script
Ruth 2:15-23

SAVING FACE

Not only did Boaz care about protecting Ruth physically, he also cared about protecting her emotionally. He was concerned enough to protect her from embarrassment, an emotion that can cause a great deal of pain and stress.

What causes that funny feeling of embarrassment to come upon you? People get embarrassed over any number of things. Wikipedia.org,[21] the online encyclopedia, offers these examples:

- losing in a competition or a bet

- demonstrating/revealing incompetence to others

- socially awkward behavior

- making unwarranted or incorrect assumptions about others

- being mistaken or making a mistake

- accidents (tripping, spilling liquids, etc.)

- having one's undergarments visible

- having private information revealed

- accompanying or being associated with someone who is behaving in an embarrassing way

    - being rejected by another person

Do you know how important people are?

A true friend will try to protect another from embarrassment, but it takes a really special person to try to save a stranger from those uncomfortable feelings. Just the other day I was in the grocery store, and there was an older woman who looked as though she had gone to great lengths to achieve her "look." She had her hair done beautifully and her face made-up perfectly, but her too-tight skirt was hiked up in the back, revealing more than I suspect she would have wanted people to see. It really needed to be pulled down, but evidently the fabric of the skirt and the fabric of her pantyhose were adhering to one another, so every time she moved, the skirt was inching its way further up her backside. Did I tell her? I truly thought about it. I was really going to. But no, I didn't. I could not bring myself to walk over to a complete stranger and tell her she needed to pull her skirt down.

Recently, Danya's basketball team had a once in a lifetime opportunity to play at the FedEx Forum in Memphis, home of the NBA's Memphis Grizzlies. The thrill of playing where basketball greats like Shaquille O'Neal and Kevin Garnett have dribbled and dunked quickly dissolved for one girl as she realized that she didn't have her complete uniform. Somehow, she had packed only her red jersey, not her red shorts. Three hours away from home, with just a few minutes before game time, there was nothing she could do about it. She had her complete white uniform with her, so she would have to wear her white shorts with her red jersey. When ninth-grader Rachael learned of her teammate's dilemma, she didn't think twice about changing into her white shorts, too, so her friend wouldn't have to be the only one in a mix-matched uniform.

Do you know how important people are? Rachael does. She was willing to do what was necessary to help another person save face. Unfortunately, we do not always take care of each other as we should, with the compassion necessary to guard not only lives but hearts as well.

Boaz could have just sent Ruth away that morning and told her he would take care of her and Naomi because they were his kin. He could have denied her the privilege of working, but he knew the value and pride Ruth would feel if she spent the day finishing the job she began. He showed even more kindness by instructing his men to drop some grain on purpose so she would have more to pick up. He cautioned them not to embarrass her. After all, I can imagine Ruth's efforts at gleaning were awkward. Her movements would have been clumsy and graceless as she went about her first day. It would have been easy to make fun of the new girl, especially since she was a Moabite.

Mary Kay Ash, the woman who started a multi-million dollar cosmetics industry, knew the significance of the individual. She was once asked the secret to her success. She replied, "Pretend that every single person you meet has a sign around his or her neck that says, 'Make me feel important.' Not only will you succeed in sales, you will succeed in life." This was her life's mission. Impossible? No—HIMpossible. For nothing is impossible with God.[22]

JOURNALING

- Describe a time when you were embarrassed. What happened?

____

____

____

____

- Is there anyway you could have "saved face"?

____

____

____

- Why is it just as important to protect people's hearts and feelings as their physical bodies?

____

____

____

- If it had been you, would you have told the lady in the grocery store to adjust her clothing? What would you have done?

____

____

____

- Make someone feel important today, a sibling, a parent, a friend, or a neighbor. Record what you did, and how it was received, here.

____

____

____

- Turn to page 152 and pray for the *Ruth* you know today.

I AM THE GOOD SHEPHERD

Read the Script
John 10:11-18, 27-28

YOU ARE CALLED BY NAME

When Jesus called Himself the Good Shepherd, it made a lot of sense to the nation of Israel. They were sheep people. For thousands of years, their country was largely used for pasture land. Sheep were a source of food for Israel, but they were valued mainly for their wool which was used for clothing and linens. Since sheep have a lifespan of about 13 years, they would endear themselves to a family and become much-loved pets, like a dog or cat would be today.

The shepherd's position embodied leadership and security. Sheep have a tendency to wander and often put themselves unexpectedly in harm's way. The shepherd protected his sheep from wild animals and dangerous situations. He often went out on a limb to rescue one of his flock. A good shepherd knew his sheep's personalities and could even recognize their faces. He could anticipate their behavior and guide them to safe places to graze. Usually, the Eastern shepherds gave names to their sheep, and they developed their own special language with them. The sheep quickly learned to recognize their names and the sound of their shepherd's voice.

When my kids were younger, we were at a McDonald's with some friends. All the girls were sitting at a table several feet away from us. We were in the crowded play area at lunch time, and it was very loud. Danya had left the girls' table, and I was trying to get the attention of her friend Olivia. I called her name several times, "Olivia! Olivia!" But she didn't hear me.

When Danya returned to the table, I called her name at the same tone and volume as I had been calling Olivia. "Danya!" Immediately, Danya looked at me.

"Yes?" Her lips formed the word from across the room. How could she hear me when Olivia couldn't? Simply put, sheep and shepherds. At the time, Danya was ten years old. For a decade, she had listened to my instructions daily. She had lived with me, eaten with me, laughed with me, and played with me. She knew my voice.

There are a lot of voices out there competing for your attention. It is easy to wander off in the wrong direction and find yourself in harm's way, in a dangerous situation.

Perhaps in our post-modern, computer driven age, it is not quite so clear to us as it was in the past, just what it means to think of God as a Shepherd. We may need to use our

--- ★ ---

He often went out on a limb to rescue one of his flock.

--- ★ ---

imaginations a little more than the ancient people of Israel needed to do. For them, the image of the Shepherd was an image of their real, contemporary world, immediately accessible, full of rich color and capable of revealing deep and meaningful truths. Still, for many of us, there is something about those biblical images of the Shepherd, such as we find in the 23rd Psalm and the 10th chapter of John's gospel. It is something that takes us home, to a place we've never actually been—or maybe we have been there, in some deep level of our spirit, the place where all human experience is shared and understood.[23]

A shepherd has a rather thankless job. He tends a flock that can never pay him back. They rest comfortably just knowing they are in his presence, and he sees to it they are well fed. Time after time, he redeems them from hazardous conditions, knowing that if push comes to shove, he will put his life on the line for the sake of his helpless charges. The shepherd protects the sheep. He prepares a way for the sheep, who could never make it on their own, to survive in the world. And because of His love—love that is undeserved and unearned—He gives the sheep a dignity and a value that they would not have otherwise.

Picture this: Jesus is your shepherd. He knows you: your personality, your face, even your tendency to wander, and He calls you by name, inviting you to know Him, too. How? Spend time with Him. Get to know Him by reading His Word, talking to Him, listening to His voice, and hanging out with His other sheep. God promises, "You will seek me and find me when you seek me with all your heart."[24] Seek the Good Shepherd, who laid down His life for you.

JOURNALING

- Read Matthew 9:36. Why did Jesus feel such great compassion for the people?

____

____

- What occupations today could be compared to shepherding? Explain.

____

____

____

- Can you picture yourself as one of Christ's sheep? What is your Good Shepherd like?

____

____

____

- Turn to page 153 and pray for the *Orpah* you know today.

REALITY CHECK WITH DANYA

UNASHAMED

Have you ever had a heart to heart conversation with your best friend where you told each other your most embarrassing moment? I know that I don't like to share things like that openly, only when I'm with one of my very best friends. And even then, we make each other promise not to tell anyone, EVER! One of my most embarrassing moments actually happened when I was with two of my best friends. I was playing a song for them on the guitar, one that I had written, and *I completely forgot the lyrics!* It wouldn't have been so bad if it had not been an original song, but this was something I had spent a lot of time on. It was one of the first songs I ever played for them, and I completely messed it up.

How many times have you been embarrassed and wished someone could have prevented it? When have you been able to prevent someone else's embarrassment? I know one time my friend saved me from potentially being known as "the pen face." I had been writing and had managed to write on myself. I don't know how, but according to her I had a nice long pen mark running down my face. I quickly wiped it off, grateful she had told me.

But how many times have you just laughed at someone else? How about the time when that girl spilled her food everywhere? Or when that guy at church tried to sing a solo and couldn't stay in tune? Or when your brother's voice changed and he squeaked when he talked? Or when your sister got a hairstyle that looked horrible? Once, I made fun of a good friend who really liked a boy that I couldn't stand. It's bad when you laugh at someone's mistake, but it's even worse when you laugh at someone's feelings.

And here's the question that has been around for a long time but applies to everything:

What would Jesus do? Would He try to protect those people, or would He laugh? Would He help them out, or would He walk away? Would He encourage them or would He be sarcastic? Jesus protects. Jesus lifts us up when we fall. Jesus encourages us to be all we can be, and Jesus calls us by name!

You know, it's a lot easier just to laugh and walk away. After all, it's not your problem, right? But in a way, it is. In Mark 12:31, Jesus says, "Love your neighbor as yourself." And in 1 Corinthians 13, definitions of love are given: Love is kind. It is not rude. It always protects.

You know, it's a lot easier just to laugh and walk away.

As Christians, it is our commandment to love our neighbors and try to protect others. Making fun of someone is not protecting them.

Have you ever been made fun of for being a Christian? Being a Christian in this day and age is not *cool*. Stepping up and acting like a Christian by standing up for someone or not going along with the crowd is like sticking a sign on your back that says, "Insult me." Many people do not like Christians. We make them feel uncomfortable. We make them feel guilty. We offend them when we stand up for what's right and don't compromise to the world's way of thinking.

Has anyone ever told you, "It's okay, your parents aren't here"? I've heard it plenty of times because I've obeyed my parents when my friends have tried to get away with stuff. I don't do it because I'm a "goody-goody" but because I know that I'm not only under my parents' authority, but I'm also under God's authority. He has commanded me to obey my parents.

The sad thing is, living under the influence of the world, we often feel embarrassed about our faith. But Jesus said in Luke 9:26, "If anyone is ashamed of me and my words, the Son of Man will be ashamed of him when He comes in His glory and in the glory of the Father and of the holy angels." This world will not last. We need to think ahead, and we need to live our lives in preparation for our future eternal home.

So, we all know what it's like to be embarrassed. We know how it feels to have people laugh at us, and we know how it feels to have someone protect us. We need to step up, be the bigger person, and start loving and protecting people. Be unashamed! It doesn't matter what the world thinks; it matters what God thinks!

JOURNALING

- Take time to complete any unanswered questions and finish up any reading you need to do for Week Five.

- Do some soul-searching about what God is teaching you. What is going on in your life, at home and with your friends?

____

____

____

____

- How can you apply the lessons you are learning?

____

____

Are you praying Jennie's prayer? How are you seeing God answer it?

____

____

____

Work on the Scripture passage you chose to memorize.

Turn to page 154 and pray for your *Boaz*.

COMING UP NEXT

THE DIRECTOR'S CHAIR

Monday
THE BOLD ONES (PART ONE)
> A PLACE TO CALL HOME

Tuesday
THE BOLD ONES (PART TWO)
> THE THRESHING FLOOR

Wednesday
GOOD ADVICE
> TAKE IT OR LEAVE IT

Thursday
PICTURE THIS
> I AM THE WAY, THE TRUTH, AND THE LIFE—YOU ARE ON COURSE

Friday
TAKE TWO
> REALITY CHECK WITH DANYA: TRUST

THE BOLD ONES (PART ONE)

Read the Script
Ruth 3:1-3

A PLACE TO CALL HOME

Despite the fact that Ruth and Naomi were able to make a way for themselves by gleaning, Naomi was troubled. She longed for Ruth to know the joy of a home and family. She longed for this daughter-in-law, this woman who had become like her own flesh and blood, to find rest in Bethlehem.

You may recall, back in chapter one, Naomi prayed for each of her daughters-in-law to find rest (or security) in the home of a husband. Let's do a quick word study to see exactly what Naomi was praying for.

Scripture	Ruth 1:9	Ruth 3:1
Hebrew word	*hxwnm*	*xwnm*
Definition	resting place	condition of rest
Used in context	Financially	emotionally

In Ruth 1:9, the Hebrew word used for rest is *hxwnm.* It is used to denote the rest that comes with financial peace. At this point in the story, chapter three, the money issue was no longer troubling Naomi. The law had taken care of her and Ruth financially by providing the opportunity to glean. Naomi was talking about a different kind of rest.

This time, the Hebrew word *xwnm* is used. The subtle difference in spelling denotes one that describes a resting place (Ruth 1:9), which would signify something material, and one that depicts a state or condition of rest (Ruth 3:1), which would indicate something intangible, having more to do with an emotion, feeling, or state of mind. *Xwnm* is used in Genesis, when Noah was adrift in the ark.

After forty days Noah opened the window he had made in the ark and sent out a raven, and it kept flying back and forth until the water had dried up from the earth. Then he sent out a dove to see if the water had receded from the surface of the ground. But the dove could find no **place to set its feet** because there was water over all the surface of the earth; so it

--- ★ ---

The dove was looking for a place to perch.

--- ★ ---

returned to Noah in the ark. He reached out his hand and took the dove and brought it back to himself in the ark. [25]

The dove was looking for a place to perch—a place to set its feet. The dove wanted *xwnm:* a resting place, a home. This was what Naomi wanted for Ruth, and she had a plan. Naomi assigned Ruth a set of detailed instructions. They sound simple enough, but a world of information is behind them.

Naomi told Ruth to do three things, bathe, anoint herself, and dress in her best clothes. First up: a bath. Hold on, don't picture a bubble bath or even a trip down to the stream! Most likely, Ruth just washed her hands, face, and feet. After this, she anointed herself with olive oil.

Olive oil was basically the wonder product of the Near East. People used it for everything.

As a **food**: Used in making bread and many other dishes.

As a **fuel**: Used in lighting lamps.

As a **cleanser**: Used as an antiseptic for wounds.

As a **drug**: Used as an ingredient in medicines.

As a **cosmetic**: Used as a styling aid for hair and makeup for skin.

Olive oil was also used to anoint prophets, priests, and kings. Throughout the Scriptures, the anointing by olive oil typically symbolized the impartation of the Holy Spirit.[26] In this case, Ruth's anointing herself was probably an indication she was no longer in a state of mourning for her husband. In other words, she was ready to marry again.

Finally, Naomi told Ruth to put on her best clothes. Naomi wanted a new life for Ruth. The garments of Ruth's past signified a broken heart, pain, sickness, and death. These belonged to Moab, not Israel. If Moab represented separation from God, Naomi wanted nothing more to do with it. She was ready to let go of the past, and she wanted Ruth to do so, as well. Because Naomi knew there *was* a kinsman-redeemer, she knew Ruth had a chance at real rest: the peace that comes from being loved, cherished, and fully accepted.

JOURNALING

Describe your home.

____

____

____

____

Is it a place where you feel loved, cherished, and fully accepted? Explain.

____

____

____

____

____

What do you like best about coming home after you have been away?

____

____

____

____

Record Matthew 11:28 here.

____

____

____

Turn to page 150 and pray for the *Mahlon* you know today.

THE BOLD ONES (PART TWO)

Read the Script

Ruth 3:4, Psalm 1

THE THRESHING FLOOR

Yesterday, we discussed the three specific directions Naomi gave Ruth concerning her personal appearance.

1.   Bathe.

2.   Anoint.

3.   Dress.

Naomi's strategy, however, was doomed without three specific elements coming together.

1.   The right place.

2.   The right time.

3.   The right man.

The *right place* was the threshing floor. On this night, it was one big party. Of course, people were working, winnowing the grain, but the atmosphere was electric with joy and enthusiasm. They were enjoying a harvest celebration only God could provide, after God had hindered it for at least a decade. The threshing floor was a busy place, with much feasting.

Naomi told Ruth to keep a low profile at this party. She did not want Boaz to know Ruth was there. Naomi knew timing was everything. She knew a man like Boaz would have work on his mind until the job was completed. Only then would he be able to relax and turn his attention to something (or someone) else. The *right time* was after the party, after the feasting, after Boaz had lain down to rest.

Boaz, the kinsman-redeemer, was the *right man*. Boaz would have been camping out at the threshing floor because it would have been sensible for him to do so. All that lovely grain would have been at risk if he was not there guarding it. Naomi knew Boaz would not have left the

--- ★ ---

She came presenting herself as a willing wife.

--- ★ ---

security of his grain to anyone but himself—he alone would accept the responsibility because that was the kind of man he was. Yes, Boaz was definitely the right man.

Naomi's bold plan also included three specific tasks for which Ruth was responsible.

1.   Note the place where Boaz lies down.

2.   Uncover his feet.

3.   Lie down there.

Then what? Naomi assured Ruth that once she finished those three tasks, Boaz would tell her what to do next.

To me, a modern day woman, this quaint little romance suddenly sounds a bit shady. Only God knows how many "love" scenes I have watched on television and at the movies, and from my culturally warped viewpoint, this looks like an act of seduction. Has Naomi lost her mind? What is going on here?

Keep in mind the time and the culture. Everything operated differently, and Naomi knew the rules. She knew, according to the law, it was up to the widow to make sure the next-of-kin carried through with the practice of kinsman-redeemer.[27] She also knew Boaz, because of the significant age difference between him and Ruth, would not approach Ruth. Understand this: Ruth was not coming to Boaz to suggest a dating relationship or even courtship. She came presenting herself as a willing wife. Her actions would remind Boaz of the duty of the kinsman-redeemer. Evidently, Naomi thought Boaz needed a bit of a nudge, a reminder that he was a candidate for Ruth's kinsman-redeemer.

As we have been studying Ruth, we have discovered the depth of character possessed by both Ruth and Boaz, and Naomi, too. To get to this point in the story and find anything dishonorable in their actions would not be in sync with the people we have come to know. The place where Boaz lay would have been some type of mat or pallet. Ruth was instructed to lie at his feet, crosswise. Both would have been fully dressed, as it was the custom to sleep in the same clothes as those worn during the day. Was this an immoral act? No. Was it risky? Yes. Why did she do it?

In a sermon on Ruth 3, Dr. Iain D. Campbell of the Back Free Church of Scotland said, "Why did [Ruth] come to follow these directives that Naomi had given her and these signposts that had pointed her to Boaz and where he was? Well, she came with a sense of great need. She came because there was nothing else that she could do. To whom else could she go? Boaz alone had the promise of security and of hope and of rest for her soul."[28]

JOURNALING

- The threshing process loosened the grain from the chaff, the husk of the grain (which was worthless). Winnowing was the final step, as a large forked tool was used to toss the grain into the air, using the wind to blow the chaff away, while the valuable grain landed in a pile. In Psalm 1, God compares the wicked to this useless chaff. Make a list below of how God describes the righteous.

____

____

____

____

____

____

- Do you see any significance in the fact that the right place for Ruth to talk to Boaz is at the threshing floor? Explain.

____

____

____

____

- Why do you think dating or courtship was not an option? Why is there so much emphasis on dating in our culture, and there wasn't back then?

____

____

____

____

- Turn to page 151 and pray for the *Naomi* you know today.

GOOD ADVICE

Read the Script
Ruth 3:5-6

TAKE IT OR LEAVE IT

Where do you go when you need some good advice? Do you take the advice you're given? The significance of the two verses you read for today lies in the fact that Ruth accepted Naomi's advice, even when it was unasked for, and she followed it to the letter. Completely.

When I was growing up, I had a good friend who lived around the corner from me, and he also went to my church. He was a few years older than I was, and to me, he was the older brother I never had. I would often go to him for advice about how to deal with issues with my friends or at school. I would listen to what he had to say, but I would still end up doing what I wanted to. In other words, I didn't follow his advice unless it was what I wanted to hear and what I already planned on doing.

One day I was asking for his advice about something and he said, "I'm not going to tell you what to do unless you promise me you will do exactly what I say."

I looked at him like he had lost his mind. "How can I possibly agree to do what you say before I know what it is?"

"Then you don't really want my advice," he said.

Hmmm. I argued for a few minutes but soon realized he had a point. I never weighed his words carefully or took his advice very seriously. I was mainly just talking about my life and hoping for someone to agree with the way I was living it. His thoughts did not truly matter. I was going to do what I wanted to do, so why should he waste his breath?

Herein lies the popularity of advice columns. Syndicated in newspapers and abounding on the Internet, these features accomplish two goals: The "expert" gives her sought-after opinion and feels good about her worldly wisdom and snappy comebacks. The seeker acquires a public forum to discuss herself and her life. Many times people write in to these "experts" because they want someone to tell them they did the right thing, or they want someone to agree with them that they have been wronged. Of course, these "experts" have problems of their own.

Naomi had earned the right to speak into Ruth's life.

Well-known advice columnists Dear Abby and Ann Landers are a good example. These women were actually twin sisters who were fiercely competitive. When one went into the advice-giving business, the other followed. The result was a sisterly feud lasting over twenty years. While they dished out heaping helpings of advice to their readers on life and relationships, they were not even speaking to each other! Here's another example: A few years ago, a best-selling book on how to make marriage succeed was written by a guy who had just gotten a divorce! And it is pretty easy to find parenting books written by "experts" who have never had any children of their own.

What about Naomi? Was she an "expert"? Naomi had earned the right to speak into Ruth's life. She certainly knew Ruth well, and she had Ruth's best interest in mind. With a lifetime of experience, Naomi possessed a deep wisdom and a reverential fear of God. When Naomi told Ruth it was time to remarry, time to cast off her mourning clothes and put on her party clothes, time to go to Boaz, Ruth followed Naomi's advice because she trusted her.

Don't you think Ruth was nervous?

Don't you imagine she was scared?

I know I would have been. Ruth was laying it all on the line. She was putting herself in a position where, as Naomi said, her fate would be determined by Boaz's response. He would either accept her or reject her. But still, Ruth didn't argue with Naomi. She did not even ask any questions. Ruth just said, "Okay, I will do what you say," and she began walking in faith, taking the steps necessary to be obedient. The rest was up to Boaz.

JOURNALING

- Where do you go for advice? Why? Have you ever wondered where the person you ask for advice goes for advice? Find out!

____

____

____

____

____

- Copy these verses in the space below: Proverbs 4:13, 15:31, and 27:6, Psalm 32:8.

____

____

____

What is the best piece of advice you have ever been given?

Turn to page 152 and pray for the *Ruth* you know today.

I AM THE WAY, THE TRUTH, AND THE LIFE

Read the Script

John 14:1-7

YOU ARE ON COURSE

I am not much of a traveler.

When I do travel, I always feel more comfortable if I have a good map with me. I like to know where I'm going. Even better than a map, however, is having someone along who knows the way. Then I can forget about the map and leave the responsibility of getting there to someone else.

When my husband and I went to New York City a few years ago, I was really concerned about traveling on the subway. I just knew we would take the wrong train, or lose our tickets, or wind up circling the city for the duration of our stay—lost forever on the subway. But Keith, an old friend of mine from college, lives in the Bronx, and I called him when we arrived in town. He met us at our hotel and took us to the subway station. He showed us how to get the right tickets, take the right train, and use the signs in order to know where we were going. With Keith showing us the way, we managed to navigate the subway system and visit everything we had wanted to see, from Central Park to Rockefeller Center to Ground Zero.

Most people want to know where they are going and how to get there. When it comes to finding God's plan for their lives, young people have a lot of questions.

What is God's will for my life?

What am I supposed to be?

What am I supposed to do?

I like to know where I'm going.

Wouldn't it be nice to have directions leading you through each twist and turn of your teen years, helping you with these challenging decisions that will affect the rest of your life? How can you know if you are on the right track and in the right place, especially when you feel all alone, without a map or a guide or even a hand to hold onto in the darkness of doubt and confusion?

But, wait a minute, you do have a map.

Thy Word is a lamp unto my feet and a light unto my path.[29]

And you do have a guide.

>*He calls his own sheep by name and leads them out.*[30]

And you do have a hand to hold onto.

>*…there is a friend who sticks closer than a brother.*[31]

When it comes to my life, I want to know where I am going and what I will be doing all the time. It is difficult for me to relax, hand over the directions to God, and just get there when we get there. That seems pretty silly of me. After all, He is the one who wrote those directions for my life! He is the One who knows where He wants me to go and who He wants me to be.

God directs His people in several ways.

The first and most important is through **His Word.** Read it! It is full of directions for living. When you make an effort to live according to God's principles, everything else will fall into place. You will find you get along easily with others, you think clearly, and you have peace in your heart. That's God's plan for your life.

God guides people directly through His **Holy Spirit.** The Holy Spirit helps you make wise decisions. He acts as a filter in your heart, sounding an alarm when you are getting too close to sin. He helps you distinguish wrong places, wrong people, and wrong situations. He also helps you understand the Bible. When you're feeling scared, lonely, or discouraged, He reminds you of God's promises. If you listen to Him, He will keep you on course.

God also uses **life's circumstances** to direct us. When Katie was looking for a summer job, she got two offers: one at the mall and one at a supermarket. She wasn't sure which job to take. She soon found out that she and her brother would be sharing a car for the summer. He worked at the mall. It would be much easier, since the two of them were sharing a vehicle, if she took the job at the mall.

Finally, God uses the **wise counsel** of others to direct his people. Be careful to whom you go for counsel, as we discussed in yesterday's lesson. God has given you parents, grandparents, and others in your life who can instruct you from their own experience. Ask! Most people are more than willing to share the things they have learned and the lessons God has used to teach them.

Picture this: Jesus is the way, the truth, and the life. No one who rides with Him will be lost or left behind. He has the directions. He knows the way! Go ahead, breathe a sign of relief! You are on course to arrive safely and on time—wherever He wants you to be.

JOURNALING

List the four ways God keeps you on course.

____

____

____

____

Have you ever felt the presence of Christ as you made your way through rough times? What was going on in your life? How did He keep you on course?

____

____

____

____

In what areas of your life do you have a hard time waiting for God to lead the way? Are you ever tempted to run ahead of Him?

____

____

____

____

In what areas of your life do you feel as though you are lagging behind God? Is there something you have been asked to do, and you keep coming up with excuses for not doing it?

____

____

____

____

Ask God to keep you on course and in step with Him.

Turn to page 153 and pray for the *Orpah* you know today.

REALITY CHECK WITH DANYA

TRUST

BarlowGirl was coming! They were doing a summer concert with Stellar Kart, and I was going! Now, I'm a BarlowGirl fanatic. I absolutely love them! I had always wanted to see them, and now I had the opportunity. I was going with some kids from my youth group, and everything had worked out perfectly! I had been listening to my BarlowGirl CDs everyday, and I had been walking around singing Stellar Kart's "Life Is Good" single. I was very excited.

But, a few days before the concert, my friend Becca's dad called us to let us know that his dad, Becca's "Pop", had passed away. Becca and I have been friends since we were very little, and our families are very close, so of course, we went straight to see them. I couldn't do much. I just sat with her outside, and we made sure our brothers didn't do anything they weren't supposed to.

The funeral was the day of the concert. I didn't say anything about it. I knew I needed to be with Becca. My daddy gave the eulogy. The service was beautiful. We stayed through the entire funeral and then went over to their house and stayed almost the whole day.

Sometimes, when God tells you to do something, it's not what you want. I didn't want to miss the concert. I didn't want "Mr. Pop" to die. There's a time for everything, and God knew that at the time of the concert, I would need to be somewhere else.

What would have been tragic is if God told me what to do and I still did what I already planned to do. I ask God everyday to lead me where He wants me to go. I pray that I would be in His will. If I still do whatever it is I want to do and ignore Him, that's like asking for advice that I'm not planning on using. God doesn't always tell me what I want to hear. Sometimes, when He speaks to me, I can't hear Him because I'm not listening for His command, I'm listening for His *confirmation*—His confirmation that I can just do whatever I want to do and He'll be behind me 100%. But that's not the case.

> *Sometimes, when God tells you to do something, it's not what you want.*

Jesus is the Way, the Truth, and the Life. If I try to do everything on my own, if I try to go my own way and do what I want, I'm not following Jesus. He is the Way. If I don't listen to His voice, if I hear what I want to hear, if I listen to the lies of the world, I'm not following Jesus. He is the Truth. If I continue in my sin, if I keep thinking I can save myself, I'm not following Jesus. He is the Life.

Putting complete trust in God is hard sometimes, but it's the only way to be in His will. Ruth had complete trust in Naomi. She followed Naomi's instructions without question. That's how we need to follow God. Even when it seems strange, or when it puts us in an uncomfortable situation, we need to do it. He has only our best interest at heart.

Jeremiah 29:11 says, "'For I know the plans I have for you,' declares the LORD, 'plans to prosper you and not to harm you, plans to give you hope and a future.'"

Trust Him. He is the Way, the Truth, and the Life. He is everything you need, and He wants to make you all you can be. Let Him put you where you need to be. Listen for His command. Let Him love you; let Him lead you.

JOURNALING

- Take time to complete any unanswered questions and finish up any reading you need to do for Week Six.

- Do some soul-searching about what God is teaching you. What is going on in your life, at home and with your friends?

____

____

____

____

- How can you apply the lessons you are learning?

____

____

____

- Are you praying Jennie's prayer? How are you seeing God answer it?

____

____

____

- Work on the Scripture passage you chose to memorize.

- Turn to page 154 and pray for your *Boaz*.

COMING UP NEXT

BEYOND TYPECASTING

Monday
COVER ME
> UNDER HIS WING

Tuesday
RICH MAN, POOR MAN
> THE RIGHT MAN

Wednesday
TALE SPIN (PART ONE)
> YOUR LINE OF DEFENSE

Thursday
PICTURE THIS
> I AM THE RESURRECTION AND THE LIFE—YOU ARE FULLY KNOWN

Friday
TAKE TWO
> REALITY CHECK WITH DANYA: RUNNING

COVER ME

Read the Script

Ruth 3:7-9

UNDER HIS WING

In the stillness of the night, Ruth took a deep breath. Her heart thumped hard within her chest. It was the right place. It was the right time. She walked over to where she had seen Boaz lie down. Then she lifted the cover from his feet, and in one careful motion, she gently lay down. She slowly exhaled a sigh of relief. She had done her part, following Naomi's instructions to the letter. The rest was up to Boaz. Would he redeem her?

Around midnight, Boaz stirred. He realized someone was lying at his feet and asked, "Who are you?"

Ruth answered bravely, "I am your servant Ruth. Spread the corner of your covering over me, since you are a kinsman-redeemer."

Ruth got right to the point with Boaz, so that no matter how dense the darkness of that midnight hour, her reason for being there was crystal clear. In fact, Ruth used a bit of wordplay, making reference to the day she and Boaz first met and reminding him of how graciously he had accepted her then. On that day, you may remember Boaz blessed Ruth with a prayer. He said, "May you be richly rewarded by the Lord, the God of Israel, under whose wings you have come to take refuge."[32] The Hebrew word for *wing* is the same as the word used for *covering*. Was Ruth daring to suggest Boaz might be the answer to his own prayer? Might he be her reward?

You may have heard the saying, "Be careful what you pray for. You just might get it!" When my friend Micca's aunt died, she prayed God would somehow soothe the pain of her uncle and cousin's broken hearts and lighten their burden. She didn't know she would be the very one God would use to bring about the answer to her prayer!

As the mourners left the funeral home, it was raining. Micca was helping her mother walk across the slick pavement. She explains:

Just as we got to the car, Mom let go of my arm and grabbed onto the car door. That's when I slipped! Both of my legs went up in the air, my dress went over my head, and I came down in a split! (I didn't even know I could do a split!)

--- ★ ---

The rest was up to Boaz. Would he redeem her?

--- ★ ---

Everyone could have ignored me, but no. They rushed to my side. I was horrified!
My mother was laughing so hard her body shook and tears ran down her face.
Finally gaining control of herself, she began to speak. I thought she would ask,
"Are you okay, honey?" Instead, she said, "Thanks, we needed that!" The crowd
began to laugh as well, with apologies, of course, between each chuckle.

As I stood there providing the entertainment, it dawned on me. This must be
God's way of giving us a break from our grief. I did ask God to lighten the
burden, but why did He have to use me? Then I remembered that it is often the
one who prays the prayer that becomes the vessel through which God works.[33]

At their first meeting, Boaz told Ruth by way of introducing himself that he knew her. He had
heard about her, and he knew her character. Now, at this midnight meeting, Boaz asked her to
identify herself. When she told him who she was, she also told him who he was. She was his
servant; he was one who *could* save her. She was in need of shelter; he was one who *could*
cover her. She was willing to be loyal to the law and to her Hebrew family; he was a kinsman-
redeemer who *could* fulfill the law. Would he?

JOURNALING

Has God ever used you to answer your own prayer?

____

____

____

____

____

Have you ever been the answer to someone else's prayer?

____

____

____

____

When you pray, are you willing for God to use you to answer your prayers? For example, if you pray for your youth group to be friendlier, are you willing to step up and lead the way? If you pray for you and your siblings to get along, are you willing to overlook minor offenses, being quick to forgive and slow to become angry?

Look up Matthew 23:37. Copy it here.

Turn to page 119 and pray for the *Mahlon* you know today.

RICH MAN, POOR MAN

Read the Script
Ruth 3:10-13

THE RIGHT MAN

Back in 1997, Joshua Harris wrote a revolutionary book entitled, *I Kissed Dating Goodbye*. In it, he chronicled his journey from a self-proclaimed "recreational dater," who pushed the limits of purity, to a guy who had a new attitude toward dating. He determined to avoid dating because he did not believe it was God's best way of doing things. He chose to go against the grain of common thinking, openly challenging the culture. The great debate he ignited has been stirring the hearts and refining the focus of young singles everywhere, ever since.

If Christians are supposed to be different from the world, then why is dating one area where we are the same? Christian kids rush into the boyfriend-girlfriend stage as early as everyone else. They are just as eager to label what should be friendships with romantic undertones. Like their secular counterparts, Christian young people are quick to give their hearts away and allow their focus to be distracted by exclusive relationships. Sadly, even some Christian girls tend to associate their self-worth with whether or not they have a boyfriend.

I was one of those girls. I believed the lie that in order to be good enough I had to be accepted by the guys, so I dated. Caught up in the romance and drama of the teen scene, I broke a few hearts and had my own broken several times. I, too, pushed what I perceived as the limits of purity, jeopardizing my Christian testimony and my relationship with the Lord, clearing the way for Satan to take a foothold in hearts I had no business trifling with. When it comes to worldly dating, I know what I'm talking about. Allow me to illustrate it this way:

> Imagine I was in an accident and you came to see me in the hospital. There are machines hooked up to my body with those weird plastic sacs dispensing medicine one drop at a time into my bloodstream. I am covered in bandages. Both legs are in casts. Both arms are in slings.
>
> "Rebecca!" you exclaim. "What happened?"
>
> "Well," I explain, "I was speeding. I was really in a hurry to get where I was going, and I just ignored all the speed limits that were posted and all the warning signs because I had somewhere I wanted to be."
>
> "Was anyone else hurt?" you ask.

When it comes to worldly dating, I know what I'm talking about.

"Unfortunately, yes," I answer quietly. "I was having so much fun speeding along that I really didn't stop to think I might hurt someone else."

"Is everyone going to be okay?"

There is a long pause before I answer. "Everyone is going to be okay, but no one will ever be the same. Please, please," I beg you, *"don't speed!"*

I think dating is like speeding. It rushes the growing up process, cheating you out of a safe, enjoyable journey. It sets up an opportunity for accidents that affect you and others. It leaves you bruised and broken, and no one is ever the same.

I'm using the Scripture you read for today as my chance to talk about dating. Boaz said it was a kindness to him that Ruth had not "run after younger men, whether rich or poor." *The Message* Bible paraphrases Boaz's words this way:

> *God bless you, my dear daughter! What a splendid expression of love! And when you could have had your pick of any of the young men around.*

Did you ever stop to think that *not dating* is a kindness—a splendid expression of love—to your future husband? Here are a few reasons why.

1. ***Not dating* guards your heart.** In fact, it preserves your heart to be given fully to your husband, with no emotional ties to anyone else.

2. ***Not dating* gives you the chance for real-time relationships.** You have the opportunity to develop some lifelong friendships with guys by being the Christian sister they need. You can encourage them in their relationship with God and help them focus on their studies, sports, hobbies, and missions. You can be a part of other people being able to look back on their teen years without regrets, but with tons of fun memories!

3. ***Not dating* protects your purity.** Josh McDowell, a noted Christian author and culture expert, conducted a study and found that the age at which dating begins is strongly connected with sexual purity.[34]

Age Dating Begins	Percent who have sex before high school graduation
12	91%
13	56%
14	53%
15	40%
16	20%

The right man. What is he worth to you? Is he worth not dating anyone else? Would you consider accepting the challenge of a radical mindset that demands more than what everyone else is doing?

My family attended a wedding a few years ago where the bride and groom had chosen to do just that. Sara and Troy had never kissed each other. They had chosen a higher standard for their dating: purity. The year they spent getting to know each other and each other's family was also spent diligently guarding each other's purity, which started by keeping their kisses for after they were married. We had a front row seat for their first kiss! It was the most exciting wedding I have ever been to.

Dating is not a biblical concept. The Old Testament culture was one of betrothals, arranged marriages established specifically to produce families and carry on lineages. That was then. This is now. Dating is a part of our cultural landscape. If you choose to do it differently, what will it look like? How do you "date" God's way?

Primarily, it's going to look more like friendship. You'll think of the guys you know as your friends, your brothers in Christ. You'll go out in groups. Besides going to the movies or the mall, you'll do things with your friends that will serve and minister to others. You'll volunteer together.

You won't be exclusive, saving all your time, energy, and emotions and investing these in one person. You won't sacrifice the relationships you have with your friends and family because someone is demanding your undivided attention. You won't play games with people's hearts. You'll protect hearts, including your own. You'll wait. You'll pray. You'll wait and pray some more. Pastor and author Tommy Nelson once said the way to find the right person is to run as hard and as fast as you can toward Jesus—then take a look at who is running beside you.

That is exactly what Ruth did. She ran for God. She followed the law of a new culture and accepted the challenge of a radical Hebrew mindset that demanded more from her. At the midnight hour she found acceptance, instruction, and blessing; this was the *right time*. She proved her virtue in lying still and waiting at the feet of the kinsman-redeemer; this was the *right man*. Remember where she found him: on the threshing floor, where the wheat (what is valuable) is separated from the chaff (what will fade away); this was the *right place*. The right time, the right man, and the right place—all three must come together, and all three will. Don't speed! God has a plan for your life.

JOURNALING

- Have you ever thought about *not dating*?

____

- How do you feel about saving your first kiss—or if you have already given that first kiss away, your *next* kiss—until your wedding day?

____

____

Get Real!

Do you think there are many guys out there who feel the same way you do?

____

____

____

What are some ways that you "run toward Jesus"?

____

____

____

If you compare dating to speeding, where is your vehicle right now? Parked in the garage, flying down the highway, or somewhere in-between? Explain.

____

____

____

____

Turn to page 151 and pray for the *Naomi* you know today.

TALE SPIN (PART ONE)

Read the Script
Ruth 3:14-18

YOUR LINE OF DEFENSE

Who are you? Quick—off the top of your head—how do you answer that question?

When Boaz asked Ruth, she answered immediately, naming herself by saying, "I am Ruth, your handmaid" (or servant). With humility, she claimed a subservient position of *belonging*. In our study, we have noticed that others have tagged her as "Ruth the Moabitess" or "Ruth, Naomi's daughter-in-law." Here, however, Boaz asked Ruth directly to identify herself, and she wanted to be known as his.

It is a good thing we readers know who everyone is at this point because this midnight visit had the power to cause lots of trouble, and Boaz knew it did. Ruth's coming to the threshing floor at this hour certainly indicated her desperate desire to know where she stood with Boaz, but the circumstances carried the potential to cause huge misunderstandings, along with the loss of two spotless reputations.

Isn't it interesting how it takes years to build a good reputation and mere seconds for it to collapse? One wrong move, one misspoken word, one bad attitude, and WHAM!—a reputation is shattered. Why is that? Is it because people would rather believe the worst about someone? Is the temptation to gossip so strong that we have no regard for the assault waged on a person's integrity? What about the consequences?

My friend Kathy was a professional musician. She played the timpani (those large kettledrums that are usually part of an orchestra). She had a great reputation among her colleagues for being not only talented, but also professional and easy to work with. Imagine her surprise when her phone suddenly stopped ringing with calls for gigs and other musicians began treating her with disdain. With her bills piling up and no work in sight, she began to pray for God to show her what was going on. Finally, a fellow musician called Kathy.

"You need to know something," he began, as he explained that Brady*, another timpanist, had been slandering Kathy's name—slowly, steadily robbing her of her reputation as well as her livelihood. He was telling lies about Kathy to the people at the symphony and other music venues and then offering to play in her place. People were afraid to work with Kathy and began giving all her gigs to Brady. What's

Kathy was one of the first ones at the hospital.

interesting is Kathy knew this guy and considered him a friend. She had no reason to think he would hurt her in such a way.

Although others suggested she go public with what Brady was doing, she refused to defend herself. She said, "At first, I was really angry. After all the years I had spent working in the music business and establishing credibility as a performer, I had nothing because of what one person was saying!

"But I came to a conclusion. If I really believed God's Word, then I believed that He was my defense. I had to trust Him to settle the matter and save my good name because I am His."

A few weeks later, Brady was involved in a severe car accident. Kathy was one of the first ones at the hospital. She sat at his bedside, praying over him and spending time with his family. With tears in his eyes, Brady asked her, "Why are you here, doing this, after everything I've done to you?" Kathy explained that because of Christ's forgiving love, she could forgive him. Brady later admitted to everyone that he had sabotaged Kathy in order to get more work, and her reputation was restored. In fact, her act of forgiveness was so amazing to the non-Christians she worked with, it gave her many more opportunities to share her faith.

A good reputation is worth guarding, and we will talk about some concrete ways to do that on Monday. Just remember, no one can control what others think or choose to believe. Leave your reputation and your character in the hands of God as He develops Christ in you. He is your defender because you are His.

JOURNALING

- Who are you?

- What kind of reputation do you have? Did you earn it, or was it given to you?

What do you do when people say untrue things about you?

____

____

____

____

If you knew someone had lied about you, could you sit back and wait on the Lord as Kathy did? What do you think about the way she responded?

____

____

____

____

Read Isaiah 53:7 and Matthew 27:12-14. How did Jesus respond to His accusers?

____

____

____

Copy Psalm 35:23 in the space below.

____

____

____

Turn to page 152 and pray for the *Ruth* you know today.

I AM THE RESURRECTION AND THE LIFE

Read the Script

John 11: 17-37

YOU ARE FULLY KNOWN

The desire to be understood is a human need. We were created with a craving to be known. This is what drives us to establish friendships and produce families. However, even in the most intimate relationships with other people, there is something missing because we can never be fully known apart from God.

Only God has been by your side every minute of every day. He has heard every word and known every thought and discerned every motive of your heart. There is no friend, no sibling, no parent—and I hate to break it to you, but in the future, no husband—who will ever completely know and understand you. Until that human desire to be fully known is met by Christ, our hearts feel abandoned, isolated, and incomplete. This is what leads every person on a search for God.

I find great comfort in the fact that even Jesus, who was both God and man, experienced loneliness while He was a resident of this planet. He lived here, "being made in human likeness, and being found in appearance as a man,"[35] for thirty-three years, and yet, He was never fully known.

- At the age of twelve, Mary and Joseph were totally baffled when they found Jesus in the temple, sitting among the teachers, listening to them and asking them questions.[36] His parents didn't know who He was.

- Twenty-one years later, Jesus' brothers didn't like the way He was managing His "campaign."[37] Although they had grown up with Him, His siblings didn't know who He was.

Only God has been by your side every minute of every day.

- Peter proclaimed Jesus was the Christ, but when Jesus began to explain that He would be crucified, Peter took Him aside and told Him He shouldn't say such things.[38] Peter didn't know who He was.

- The Pharisees and the teachers of the Law had supposedly been preparing for the Messiah's arrival all of their lives, but when Christ appeared, they crucified Him. They didn't know who He was.

Do you ever feel like nobody knows who you really are? Like nobody "gets" you? That can hurt. Whether it is a friend who wrongly accuses you, or a family member who doesn't realize you're not a kid anymore, or an adult who typecasts you because of the way you dress, it can be terribly painful to be misunderstood. I've certainly cried my share of tears over those wounds.

In today's Scripture you read of Christ's tears. Many people believe Jesus cried because He was mourning the death of Lazarus. They think it was Christ's compassionate heart causing Him to grieve along with the sisters, Mary and Martha. However, if you take a closer look at this passage, you may come to a different conclusion.

Jesus knew He was going to raise Lazarus from the dead. When He first heard of Lazarus's illness, Jesus told His disciples it would not end in death, but God's Son would be glorified by it.[39] Why would Jesus grieve over Lazarus' death when He knew He was going to resurrect him? I believe Christ was weeping over the people's unbelief. After all the time Jesus had spent with His good friends Mary and Martha, they still didn't really know Him.

Picture this: Jesus has a spotless reputation. His name is impeccable. Everything the Bible says about Him is true, and yet, despite what we know about Him and what we say we believe, there are areas of our lives revealing our doubts. Do you fully trust Him? He is fully trustworthy. Do you believe He is the Son of God who died on a cross to pay for your sins? Do you believe He covers you with His blood? Do you believe He longs to be fully known, even as He fully knows you? He is your life. Live it!

JOURNALING

Do you ever feel lonely?

____

____

____

Is there anyone in your life who really understands you?

____

____

____

What was Mary and Martha's view of death? Temporary or permanent? Explain.

____

Get Real!

◢ Why did it not occur to them that Jesus would be able to heal Lazarus no matter when He came? Who did they think Jesus was?

____

____

____

____

◢ Who do you say Jesus is?

____

____

____

____

◢ Turn to page 153 and pray for the *Orpah* you know today.

REALITY CHECK WITH DANYA

RUNNING

I had been building my reputation around my friends for a long time. I was the good girl, the one who never disobeyed her parents, the one who always got good grades in school, the one who knew all the answers to the questions in Sunday school, and I hated it. I hated it because some of them made fun of me for it, and some of them had stopped being my friend because I was too "good."

Then one night, our youth group was in the church van traveling to a Christmas party, and a girl sitting in front of me suddenly turned around and started yelling at me! She was very loud and very accusing, and I had no idea why. As I sat there listening, trying to decide whether or not to defend myself, I noticed that no one else was paying any attention to this girl. The only one who appeared to have even noticed that this girl was talking was my friend Laura*, who was trying to keep from laughing. My reputation saved me that night. No one believed this girl. They were all ready to defend me. I never hated my reputation again.

What was strange to me was that this girl had known me for a long time, and she still didn't *really* know me. Only one person could ever fully know me: Jesus.

Tommy Nelson's quote is a quote to live by. Run as hard and as fast as you can towards Jesus, the One who can fully know you. Then, without slowing down, look and see who's running beside you. Right now, there might not be anyone running beside you. That's the sacrifice we have to make. We have to be willing to follow Jesus, to leave everything and everyone else behind, and we have to be willing to do it even if no one else is. We have to be willing to be *different.*

One of the ways we can be different is by not dating the world's way, but by dating God's way. As for me, I would rather have the reputation of being God-crazy than being boy-crazy.

I want to run to God.

I have a lot of friends who are guys. They're really great people, and they're a lot of fun to hang out with and talk to. Guys can be a lot more realistic than girls. They can give you different opinions and show you things you wouldn't have seen otherwise. They can be really great friends, too.

I've decided not to date until I'm ready to consider marriage. I'm not saying that's what you should do, but that's what I'm doing. I've seen many of my friends get their hearts broken by guys. When you start a relationship before you're ready to consider marriage, it's pointless. You can have fun with guys and have close friendships with guys without dating. Even when I start to think I like one of my guy-friends as more than a friend, I don't act on it. The feeling eventually passes, which proves it wasn't love, it was just a crush. I've wondered how some of my friends can have one boyfriend one week and a different one the next. It's because the feelings are temporary and it's not love.

When I focus on protecting and maintaining a friendship, I don't have to go through a break-up. My heart isn't broken, and I don't have to break someone else's. We girls can get very mean sometimes, and we can say things and do things that can scar people for a long time. By not dating, and then not having to break up, I get to keep the friendship and there are no awkward moments or hurt feelings.

I also think about the future. I want to be a friend to my guy-friends even after they're married. I want to be friends with their wives. I don't want any regrets. I want to be a heart-protector.

I want to live for God. I want to run to God. I want to be all about God, living a radical, different, lifestyle that mirrors my Savior. Then, I will look to see who's running beside me. I hope you will, too.

JOURNALING

- Take time to complete any unanswered questions and finish up any reading you need to do for Week Seven.

- Do some soul-searching about what God is teaching you. What is going on in your life, at home and with your friends?

____

____

____

____

- How can you apply the lessons you are learning?

____

____

____

Are you praying Jennie's prayer? How are you seeing God answer it?

____

____

____

Work on the Scripture passage you chose to memorize.

Turn to page 154 and pray for your *Boaz*.

COMING UP NEXT

THE REALITY SHOW

Monday
TALE SPIN (PART TWO)
GUARDING YOUR REPUTATION

Tuesday
DEAL OR NO DEAL
MORE THAN WILLING

Wednesday
FAMILY AFFAIR
BLESSING THE BRIDE

Thursday
PICTURE THIS
I AM THE TRUE VINE—YOU ARE THE BRANCHES

Friday
TAKE TWO
REALITY CHECK WITH DANYA: CAUGHT

TALE SPIN (PART TWO)

Read the Script

Ruth 3:14-18 (Read it again!), I Timothy 4:12

GUARDING YOUR REPUTATION

"Don't let your good be evil spoken of," my mother often said as I was growing up. While it is true you will never be able to control what others think, when it comes to guarding your reputation, there are a few things you can do to protect yourself and your good name. That's really all Boaz was trying to do as he sent Ruth on her way before dawn broke over Bethlehem. He knew nothing sinful had gone on between them. He knew Ruth came to him in humility and not in an effort to seduce him. Others would not know that. He respected the importance of the way things appear. The places you go, the clothes you wear, and the people you are with say a great deal about the young woman you are.

The places you go. My friend Robby was really upset when his youth pastor, Tom, called him in for a private meeting. Tom told Robby that he had received a call from a girl who saw him drinking at a party. Tom was upset for several different reasons, but especially because Robby was a student leader and he had set a bad example for this girl, who had just begun visiting our church. Robby explained to Tom that yes, he had been at the party, but no, he had not been drinking. Tom explained to Robby that simply because he was present at this kind of party, the people who were there to drink would assume that he was there to drink, too. Tom warned Robby rumors were easily started, and Robby's Christian reputation could be severely damaged.

The clothes you wear. If you want to guard your reputation, it's important to be aware of what your clothes are saying about you. Many young women enjoy wearing the latest fashions. Unfortunately, many of those fashionable clothes can provoke sexual thoughts in a young man's mind.

Here's the truth: Girls can look at a handsome young man and simply admire him. We think he's cute. We might desire his attention. For the most part, our thoughts don't wander too far from that. But guys are visually stimulated. When a young man sees a girl in revealing clothing, his thoughts are at risk for reeling into lust almost before he can realize it. There is nothing "cute" about these thoughts. Satan quickly attacks a guy's mind with pornographic images and sexual desires.

He respected the importance of the way things appear.

What is considered revealing clothing? Here's the list at my house:

- Shoulder-baring dresses and tops

- Navel-baring tops

- Shirts that dip down and expose cleavage or the place where your breasts begin to curve

- Too tight clothes

- Too short shorts

My friend Marilyn Morris, who teaches abstinence in schools around the country, says there are three reasons why a girl chooses to dress immodestly:

1. **She's uninformed.** It's possible no one has taken the time to educate her about what goes on in a young man's mind when he sees a girl dressed immodestly.

2. **She's a tease.** Some girls are fully aware of what they are doing. They enjoy the power trip they get from teasing the boys around them. This is cruel, manipulative, and sinful.

3. **She's easy.** Some girls dress immodestly because they are inviting boys to think of them as being available for a sexual relationship. They are advertising.

How is a young man supposed to know which of these categories a girl falls into? According to Marilyn, most guys will put a girl in the category that best suites his desires. This is exactly how many girls have found themselves in dangerous situations. Girls need to understand the way they dress makes a strong statement to the opposite sex about who they are, and it can quickly brand their reputation.

The people you're with. In the 18th century, George Washington said, "Associate yourself with men of good quality if you esteem your own reputation; for 'tis better to be alone than in bad company." When my mom was a teen, they said, "Birds of a feather flock together." And when I was in high school, we said, "You are who you hang with." People associate you with your friends.

It is really important to be kind and loving toward everyone you meet, but when you are choosing the friends you spend the most time with, choose wisely. Look for friends who love the Lord and seek Him first. Connect with people who have the kind of relationship with Christ that will challenge you to a higher standard in your walk with Him.

At the same time, it is important to imitate Christ and love those who are hard to love. Be intentional about establishing friendships with those God puts in your path that need to see Jesus in you.

Appearances definitely matter, but don't confuse that with giving a false impression. You want to be real. Jesus challenged us to let our light shine before men so they may see our good deeds and praise our Father in Heaven.[40] There is a fine line between being a God-pleaser and being a man-pleaser. Sometimes, people want to look good before others as a matter of pride. Then they are not really guarding their reputation, they are simply putting on a good show.

JOURNALING

How can you guard your reputation in these areas? Do you need to make some changes?

The things you say (or don't say)

____

____

____

The places you go

____

____

____

The movies you see

____

____

____

The music you listen to

____

____

____

The clothes you wear

____

____

Get Real!

The friends you choose

____

____

Read Ruth 3:18 again. How did Naomi know Boaz would settle the matter that day?

____

____

Protecting someone else's reputation, guarding her name, is a way of caring for another. Boaz cared for Ruth in this way. How can you care for someone else's reputation?

____

____

____

Find Proverbs 22:1. What did King Solomon mean by this verse? Is it still true today?

____

____

____

Turn to page 150 and pray for the *Mahlon* you know today.

DEAL OR NO DEAL?

Read the Script
Ruth 4:1-8

MORE THAN WILLING

Four things were required in order for a kinsman to redeem:[41]

1.   He must be near of kin.

2.   He must be able to redeem.

3.   He must be willing to redeem.

4.   He must pay the price completely.

Boaz was inhibited by only one thing: There was someone who was a nearer relative. If that person met all four of the requirements, he could redeem Ruth.

Boaz was quite the shrewd businessman. He knew how to conduct business dealings, and he knew how to handle people. Boaz knew he could find the man he was looking for at the town gate, which was something like today's city hall. Business transactions were conducted there regularly. Boaz informed the nearer kinsman that Naomi had property to sell and that he had the right to purchase it. Initially, the man was gung-ho about claiming the property. Then wise Boaz got to the point: Ruth the Moabitess was part of the deal. If he bought the property, he must agree to marry her and to have a child with her who would receive Mahlon's inheritance. This made a difference to the man, and he refused. He was near of kin. He was able. But he was not willing.

How often are we able to do something good, but we are not willing? Josh and Kara*, the parents of two toddlers, were thrilled when Josh got a promotion at work that allowed them to move from their cramped two-bedroom apartment into a roomier three-bedroom one. They had barely gotten settled when word began circulating in our church that a pregnant teen in our community had been kicked out by her parents and needed a place to live. The baby was due any day. Our suburban church was full of people who had comfortable homes with plenty of room to shelter a mother and child, yet in spite of so many who were able, none were willing. Josh and Kara gave up the extra space they had desired for so long to accommodate this mother and child. They were barely able, but they were more than willing.

-- ⭐ --

Ruth the Moabitess was part of the deal.

-- ⭐ --

Perhaps, like the nearer kinsman, we go along with something while it suits our interests and then back off when it becomes inconvenient or troublesome. A job promotion and the extra money that comes with it sound good until you realize there is more work and responsibility involved. Being part of a team and looking cool in the uniform is appealing until you have to practice five nights a week. Playing in a band seems great until you grasp the fact that it takes years of committed training offstage before you get to be in the spotlight. Even friendships can be difficult. Lots of people are willing to share the laughter and good times, but they bail out when it comes to bearing one another's burdens.

Take another look at today's script. What's missing? I hope you noticed it in the very first verse you read.

> Meanwhile Boaz went up to the town gate and sat there. When the kinsman-redeemer he had mentioned came along, Boaz said, "Come over here, my friend, and sit down." So he went over and sat down."[42]

The *name* of this nearer kinsman is missing! In a book filled with meaningful names, this man's is glaringly absent. Get this: What the NIV and other contemporary versions translate as "friend" is more literally translated as, "a certain man" or more understandably, "so and so." Bible scholar Matthew Henry believes this is an intentional snub by the author of Ruth. He says, "[Boaz] called him by his name, no doubt, but the divine historian thought not fit to record it, for, because he refused to raise up the name of the dead, he deserved not to have his name preserved to future ages in this history."[43]

While Boaz is famous forever as *in him is strength* and Ruth will always be celebrated as *friend,* this man is known throughout history as *able but not willing,* the man who refused to redeem.

JOURNALING

Have you ever considered that you might be sinning against God for what you haven't done? Copy James 4:17 in the space below.

____

____

____

____

When it comes to being willing to do something for someone else, what motivates you? Do you act in an effort to glorify God or to get attention for yourself? Be honest.

____

____

____

____

____

____

Are you taking advantage of the opportunities God gives you to do good for others? Pray Galatians 6:10, asking God for more opportunities to do good things for Him. Write your prayer in the space below.

____

____

____

____

Turn to page 151 and pray for the *Naomi* you know today.

NOW PLAYING: FAMILY AFFAIR

Read the Script
Ruth 4:9-12, Genesis 38

BLESSING THE BRIDE

It was a hushed and holy moment that exploded into a deafening declaration of love when Boaz announced he had purchased Naomi's property and acquired Ruth as his wife. He was the kinsman-redeemer, and it was no secret. He conducted all his business live and loud so Bethlehem would know there was a goel who fulfilled all the requirements and who paid the price completely!

What followed was natural for the Israelites. They prayed blessings upon the happy couple. They prayed first for Ruth to bear children, referring to the traditional Hebrew blessing of Rachel and Leah, Jacob's wives and the mothers of his twelve sons. But then, they brought up Tamar and her scandalous role in Israel's history. Why? Genesis 38 is, well, *embarrassing*. The story of Tamar and Judah both fascinates and disgusts. Let's take a closer look. There are several intriguing parallels in these two women's stories.

Tamar's Story	Ruth's Story
Judah left Israel to live outside its borders	Elimelech left Israel to live outside its borders
Judah's two sons entered into a Gentile marriage (to the Canaanite Tamar)	Elimelech's two sons entered into Gentile marriages (to the Moabitesses Ruth and Orpah)
Judah's sons died childless	Elimelech's sons died childless
The Levirate Law of the Kinsman-Redeemer is enacted	The Levirate Law of the Kinsman-Redeemer is enacted
The first in line to redeem refuses	The first in line to redeem refuses
Out of desperation, Tamar acted out a bold plan	Out of desperation, Ruth acted out a bold plan
Tamar chose a time of celebration (sheep-shearing) to approach Judah	Ruth chose a time of celebration (harvest) to approach Boaz
Mentioned by name in the lineage of Christ (Matthew 1)	Mentioned by name in the lineage of Christ (Matthew 1)

The Bethlehemites may have been reminded of Tamar, a foreigner in need of a kinsman-redeemer, as they watched the romance of Ruth and Boaz play out. Well-acquainted with the tabloid aspects of the story, they knew all the details: Tamar, wronged by those who were supposed to uphold the Levirate law, Onan and Judah, resorted to playing the part of a prostitute in order to have a child. In her desperation, she came up with a plan which, in her mind, righted the wrongs that had been inflicted on her. Sadly, however, it was a sinful act on the part of both participants.

Judah, living outside Israel's borders and getting involved with Canaanites, had strayed far from Jehovah. He was wrong to withhold his third son from a marriage to Tamar and wrong to believe she was responsible for the deaths of his other two sons. (Their own sins before God caused their lives to be shortened.) As a widower, Judah continued to rebel against Jehovah when he sought the services of a prostitute rather than practicing godly self-control. Add to his sin tally fornication, the act of sex outside marriage.

Yet in spite of all their sins, God opened Tamar's womb. You see, the line of the Messiah was to come through Judah. In his misguided attempt to protect his third son from Tamar, Judah was standing in the way of God's plan, which was far bigger than he was. Dr. Iain Campbell explains, "Even [though] she had sinned, Tamar was fulfilling God's purpose, and Judah had to admit that she was more righteous than [he was]. From their offspring, the result of an illicit union, came Perez, the great-great-great-great-grandfather of Boaz!"[44] That does not mean their sin was justified. It simply shows God's grace doing the work the Law refused to do. The blessing of Tamar was the blessing of being drawn into a covenant relationship with God and being given a place in the lineage of the Messiah. It was the blessing of redemption.

JOURNALING

- Did Tamar or Ruth do anything to "earn" their spot in the lineage of Christ? How did they get it?

____

____

____

- Looking at the list of sins of Judah and Tamar, do you think they deserved to be a part of Christ's lineage?

____

____

____

How do you feel knowing that God's grace covered their sins?

____

____

____

____

How would you respond to someone who believes God could never accept her because of the things she has done?

____

____

____

____

Turn to page 152 and pray for the *Ruth* you know today.

I AM THE VINE

Read the Script
John 15:1-8

YOU ARE THE BRANCHES

What would Jesus eat for breakfast?

Matthew tells the story of a morning when Jesus was hungry for something to eat. Seeing a lone fig tree alongside the road, He approached it anticipating a breakfast of figs. When He got to the tree, there was nothing but fig leaves. He said, "No more figs from this tree—ever!" The fig tree withered on the spot, a dry stick.[45] The tree was pretending to be something it wasn't. It appeared to have fruit. From a distance, its thick leaves indicated figs were there. Upon closer inspection, however, there were none to be found.

Many who study the Bible believe Christ cursed the tree not because he was upset about His empty stomach, but in order to prove a point to His disciples, who were always watching Him. If you appear to have fruit but you really don't, you might look lovely from a distance. The Lord, however, knows the truth. Putting on a good show doesn't cut it with Him.

I think it's remarkable that the King of kings didn't choose to identify with a strong tree and its branches. He gave us the word picture of a vine. The disciples would have been reminded of Old Testament passages about vines. For example, a fruitful vine was often used as an illustration of a woman in her child-bearing years. Also, the prophet Isaiah said Israel was God's vine. In their daily lives, the disciples knew firsthand of a vine's ability to spread rapidly and even take over other plants with its excessive growth. And what about its branches? These are the vine's fruit-producers. A grapevine, for example, produces clusters of six to three hundred grapes, in all colors: black, blue, golden, green, purple, red, pink, brown, peach or white.[46]

Many scandals have resulted from Christians—or those who claimed to be Christians—who failed to produce fruit. Like the fig tree, they looked great from a distance. They had a reputation of fruitfulness, but upon closer inspection, no real fruit was found.

It can be terribly difficult when people let you down, whether they are "celebrity" Christians or people you know personally. In 1987, I had spent the evening weeping with one of my friends who had just found out she was pregnant. She was 19 years old. Her boyfriend was known as a godly guy on our campus. This young Christian couple, with their vibrant personalities and enthusiasm for Christ, had been a testimony to many students.

--- ⭐ ---

Putting on a good show doesn't cut it with Him.

--- ⭐ ---

As I returned to my dorm room that night, I glanced at the television only to see the late-breaking news of a prominent Christian evangelist's fall from grace—he had been involved in sexual sin. I fell to my knees unable to cope with the overwhelming feeling of being let down—in my own world and in the world at large.

I've seen favorite Christian authors and recording artists involved in ungodly affairs, resulting in divorce and broken homes. Once, a staff member at the church I attended was arrested for criminal behavior, and it was splashed across the front page of every local newspaper. The world loves it when a well-known Christian gets in trouble. The media races to convict all of us of hypocrisy. I guess I could sit around in a state of shock, shaking my head and wondering why godly people fall, but what I would rather do is look at all the godly people I know who stand for Jesus and consider what keeps them upright.

My dad has a regular time of prayer every morning. My friend Sondra attends a weekly group Bible study and makes time for personal Bible study every day. My husband Rich meets with two small groups each week. In one group, he is the mentor. In the other group, he is being mentored. Each of these examples showcases a life spent abiding in the vine. Prayer, Bible study, and relationships that allow opportunities for accountability as well as ministry are fundamentals of a close, fruit-producing walk with Jesus.

Picture this: A grapevine's job is to produce grapes. A fig tree's job is to produce figs. As a Christian, it is your job to produce fruit, too. What should your fruit look like? It should look like the Vine: Jesus.

JOURNALING

- Read Galatians 5:22-26. List the nine fruits of the Spirit.

____

____

____

- Get real: How can you stay close to the vine? List some practical ways.

____

____

____

____

____

Are you bearing fruit? Prayerfully look at your life and ask God to show you areas where you are producing good fruit (such as in your conversation, in ministry, or in your relationships).

____

____

____

Do you have places in your life that look fruity but really aren't? Are you guilty of putting on a good show? Confess your sin to God and ask Him to prune away the branches that aren't producing fruit and grow His Son's likeness in their place.

____

____

____

Turn to page 153 and pray for the *Orpah* you know today.

REALITY CHECK WITH DANYA

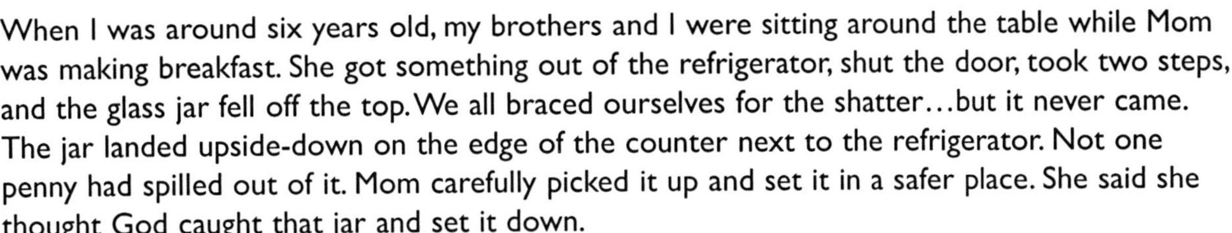

CAUGHT

Have you ever broken something made of glass? Glass is strong, but once something hits it, it shatters into a million pieces. I dropped a glass cup once while unloading the dishwasher, and it broke into several pieces. Now, imagine a glass jar sitting on top of a refrigerator, filled to the brim with pennies.

When I was around six years old, my brothers and I were sitting around the table while Mom was making breakfast. She got something out of the refrigerator, shut the door, took two steps, and the glass jar fell off the top. We all braced ourselves for the shatter…but it never came. The jar landed upside-down on the edge of the counter next to the refrigerator. Not one penny had spilled out of it. Mom carefully picked it up and set it in a safer place. She said she thought God caught that jar and set it down.

As a six-year-old, I completely believed that God had caught the jar. As a fifteen-year-old, I still believe God caught the jar. But it has a much bigger impact on me now than it did then. As I think about what a dangerous position the jar was in, full of things that would make it fall faster, I think about Tamar…Rahab…Ruth…They were all in dangerous positions. Tamar let herself become a prostitute; Rahab made a living being a prostitute. Ruth was living in a heathen nation, surrounded by sin. Their lives were full of things that would make them fall faster. But each one of these women found God.

I was talking with one of my friends recently, and as we talked, I wanted to cry. She told me about a lot of things that had happened to her. She had done just about everything you could do. Her purity had been compromised, she had tried drinking, she had been involved with drugs, and she had attempted suicide. In real life, sometimes these stories don't have happy endings. She's still lost. She's still struggling, and she's still fighting God. She's falling. But I completely believe God can catch her.

As I view my life, I wonder if, during those precious few hours I get to see my friend at church, I'm being a reflection of Jesus. I wonder if I'm being the friend I need to be. I wonder if I love her the way Jesus would love her. Is my reputation like Christ's?

I pray that I am mirroring my Savior with my life, that I'm not just putting on a hypocritical show. I pray that I am producing the fruit of the Spirit: love, joy, peace, patience, kindness, goodness, faithfulness, gentleness, and self-control. I pray I look like the Vine. I also pray that the fruit of the Vine would spread rapidly throughout my life and the lives of others, changing the way people think and act.

In John 15, Jesus said, "You do not belong to the world, but I have chosen you out of the world."

If we are not of this world, why do we try so hard to fit in? Why do we run after the latest fashions and pleasures the world offers? For Christians, this life is the prelude to eternity! God has caught us! There is so much more to come. It's time to step up and be who we were meant to be.

JOURNALING

- Take time to complete any unanswered questions and finish up any reading you need to do for Week Eight.

- Do some soul-searching about what God is teaching you. What is going on in your life, at home and with your friends?

____

____

____

____

- How can you apply the lessons you are learning?

____

____

____

____

- Are you praying Jennie's prayer? How are you seeing God answer it?

____

____

____

____

- Work on the Scripture passage you chose to memorize.

- Turn to page 154 and pray for your *Boaz*.

COMING UP NEXT

IN LIVING COLOR

Monday
A BABY STORY
> GET REAL!

Tuesday
EXTREME MAKEOVER
> NAOMI HAS A SON

Wednesday
FAMILY TIES
> INHERITED

Thursday
PICTURE THIS
> I AM—YOU ARE

Friday
TAKE TWO
> REALITY CHECK WITH DANYA: HIM

A BABY STORY

Read the Script
Ruth 4:13, Luke 1:26-38

GET REAL!

A few years ago, a young teen was playing the role of Mary in our choir's Christmas musical. She was a pretty girl with a powerful voice. Week after week as we practiced, I couldn't get over how much she looked like I had always imagined Mary looked: around 15 or 16 years old, with long brown hair, strong features, and olive-toned skin.

On opening night, about a week before Christmas, the church was full. "Mary" appeared onstage, cowering at the angel Gabriel's brilliant light as he revealed God's plan and purpose in choosing her to be the mother of the Messiah. Incredibly, our "Mary" looked authentically frightened and sincerely amazed at the news. This precious teenager then opened her mouth to sing, and the talented girl who had rendered flawless performances at every rehearsal, faltered. Stumbling over the music and the words, she was overcome with emotion and tears, sinking to her knees in genuine worship. In that moment, I came face to face with the true character of this one who agreed to be a handmaiden of the Lord. Mary was just a young teen, an ordinary person—prone to failure, weak-kneed, insecure—like the rest of us. Unbelievably, God wrapped His priceless gift of Jesus in the fragile tissue paper of an adolescent womb.

This week we are heading toward the conclusion of our study in the book of Ruth. I pray you haven't missed the reality of God's Word. God doesn't hide the truth. He doesn't camouflage people's blemishes with cover stick and powder. He exposes personalities, pain, and problems because that's real life, and that's what He calls us to live. When the going got tough, Elimelech bailed out. When Naomi's life fell apart, she became bitter. When given a choice, Orpah returned to Moab. Get real! God is not telling fairy tales! Rahab was a prostitute, Judah was a cheat, and Tamar was a manipulator. God drew them to Himself and used them in His service anyway. The apostle Paul explained it like this:

> Now remember what you were, my friends, when God called you. From the human point of view few of you were wise or powerful or of high social standing. God purposely chose what the world considers nonsense in order to shame the wise, and He chose what the world considers weak in order to shame the powerful. He chose what the world looks down on and despises and thinks is nothing, in order to destroy what the world thinks is important.[47]

God is not telling fairy tales!

What does the world think is important? Financial success. Physical beauty. Political power.
What does God think is important? Loving His Son. Loving your neighbor. Being obedient.

Crazy, huh?

In a world that is all about self, God says it's all about serving.

Servanthood ties Ruth to Mary, and Mary to Ruth. As Ruth lay at the feet of her kinsman-
redeemer, she identified herself as his handmaid, his servant. These were Mary's words, as well,
kneeling at the voice of the Lord. Ruth gave birth to Obed, whose name means, "servant." Mary
gave birth to the One who took on the very nature of a servant—the King of kings, who came
to serve. The lesson of Ruth, the message of Christmas, and the foundation of our faith is
servanthood. Selflessness. Putting others first. No wonder we fail so miserably. We will continue
to miss it until we understand it's not about us! Ruth and Mary agreed to a life of service—
they "got" it! The Moabite widow and the teenage girl understood a concept most people
cannot wrap their heads around, and in submitting to what many would believe was less, gained
much.

JOURNALING

- Speaking practically, what does servanthood look like?

____

____

____

- Why did Ruth name her son, the son of wealthy and prosperous Boaz, "servant"?

____

____

____

- How does God destroy what the world thinks is important by the people He chooses to
  participate in His plan?

____

____

____

Do you know any modern-day servants? Name names and explain how they serve in the space below.

____

____

____

____

____

____

Turn to page 150 and pray for the *Mahlon* you know today.

EXTREME MAKEOVER

Read the Script
Ruth 4:14-17

NAOMI HAS A SON

We girls are so quick to connect who we are with how we look. We're guilty of measuring others by their appearance, as well. In a culture where few people are satisfied with their appearance, makeovers are big business with big promises: A new haircut can change your outlook, the right clothes can nab a better job, and cosmetic surgery can transform your life. Big promises, but no guarantees. Read Tonya Ruiz's story below.

A Spiritual Makeover
By Tonya Ruiz[48]

As a scrawny 12-year-old, I believed if I was beautiful, my life would be perfect.

Fast forward four years—at 16, I was chosen from more than 200 girls to go to Paris and become a fashion model. My agent told me, "Your rail-thin body, shiny blond hair and sky blue eyes will be your passport to success."

My glamorous life was filled with dancing, drinking, dating, and parties. Life was a thrill a minute! It never occurred to me that my excessive eating and drinking could affect how I looked. At the modeling agency I was told, "You look puffy and tired!"

I had a whopping 120 pounds on my 5 foot 7 ½ inch frame. That was ten more pounds than I weighed in the fabulous pictures that filled my modeling portfolio. The traitorous pounds that made my face look puffy were keeping me from my dream of becoming a supermodel.

Somewhere along the way, I had lost sight of what was true.

By any normal person's standards, I would have been considered thin, but not by the fashion industry's standards and certainly not by my New York agent Eileen Ford's. One day, after a week-long fast, I walked into the agency and said, "Eileen, look, I've lost weight." I was 118 pounds. She looked me over and bluntly said, "You're still fat. Lose five more pounds."

I was consumed with the way I looked. When I scrutinized my appearance, it was like looking in a fun house mirror. My view was distorted—what was real was not what I saw. Somewhere along the way, I had lost sight of what was true. My value, both to my agents and myself, was measured by the way I looked. Since I could not look perfect, I felt worthless.

During the next two years, I traveled 75,000 miles as a fashion model. I used food, alcohol, drugs, and men to try to fill an empty place in my life. I explored various philosophies, read self-help books, and consulted my horoscope daily, searching for answers. But I did not find any. At the ripe old age of 18, I concluded that suicide was my only option. I flew home from Switzerland to say goodbye to my family before I killed myself. A few weeks after I got home, a friend of mine called and invited me to church. The night before we went, she told me about Jesus.

"First, I need to get my life cleaned up, and then I'll accept the Lord," I told her.

"Accept the Lord first," she encouraged me. "He'll help you clean up your life."

The next morning the pastor asked, "Do you have a void in your life? Have you tried everything and still feel empty? God so loved the world that He gave His only begotten Son. If you believe in Him you won't perish but have everlasting life. Do you want everlasting life? Would you like your empty life to be full of meaning?"

I felt that he was speaking directly to me. No matter what I had accomplished or acquired, I was constantly searching for that missing part of my life. I wondered, *How did he know so much about me?* I had never heard anyone explain the truth and how to become a Christian so simply. He talked about how I could receive Christ into my life—and that's exactly what I wanted to do. I realized He died for me. I accepted the Lord, and from then on, my journey took a new direction. God healed me physically and emotionally. When I stopped dieting and abusing my body with drugs and alcohol, I actually became healthy.

Today, I know physical beauty is only skin deep, but true beauty is soul deep. I rest in the fact that God does not accept me because of my jean size, the condition of my skin, or my reflection in the mirror, but because He loves me. He sent His only Son to die for me! I am, indeed, valuable to Him.

When it comes to makeovers, people focus on two things: creating a new life for themselves and reversing the effects of time. Naomi's story tells us this is only accomplished by a kinsman-redeemer. You see, if anyone required a makeover, it was Naomi. She looked so terrible entering Bethlehem that her friends did not recognize her! She had lost her hope. Her view of God was distorted. She didn't know what was true anymore. Would a facial or a manicure or a day at the spa fix that? No, but a kinsman-redeemer would.

Holding Obed in her arms and drawing him to her heart, Naomi experiences renewed life. It's a picture of what happens when you ask Jesus Christ to come into your heart: an extreme makeover. Guaranteed.

JOURNALING

- How much emphasis do you put on your appearance? Do you spend a lot of time wishing you were prettier?

____

____

____

- Tonya Ruiz thought life would be better if she were beautiful. What did she learn?

____

____

- Naomi thought life would be better if she had a kinsman-redeemer. What did she learn?

____

____

____

- Compare the townswomen's reaction to Obed's birth with their reaction to Naomi's homecoming in chapter 1.

____

____

____

- Why do they say Naomi has a son when he is actually Ruth's son?

____

____

- Have you accepted Christ's offer of an extreme makeover? If not, what are you waiting for? Ask God to forgive you of your sins, and ask Christ to come into your heart right now. Don't wait another minute.

- Turn to page 151 and pray for the *Naomi* you know today.

FAMILY TIES

Read the Script
Ruth 4:18-22, Ephesians 1:1-14

INHERITED

Several years ago, when my grandfather died, he left me some money. Talk about a surprise! Life changing? No, but it was a good amount, and there were a number of things my young family could have done with it at that time. Because the money came from my Papaw, however, I wanted to honor him in some way with it. I didn't want to save it, and I didn't want to use it to pay bills. So I prayed about it and talked it over with my husband, and finally, I settled on using the money to buy a piano. Both my grandparents loved music and sang in their church choir. I knew every time I looked at the piano, I would think of them. I knew every time I played it, and as my children learned to play, Papaw's legacy of music would continue through my family.

I had no idea I stood to gain an inheritance upon my Papaw's death. I had not asked for it, and I had not done anything to earn it. He gave it to me out of his wealth because we were family.

The great building blocks of God are families. He created humanity with family in mind: first Adam, then Eve, then children. The cycle begins. Children grow up and have families of their own. As people pass on, they leave an inheritance to their children. The Jewish people knew the importance of the inheritance, of keeping a person's property and wealth within the family line. It was a way of taking care of one's family and adding to the prosperity of the next generation. It was a way to live on, even after death.

When Ruth married Mahlon, she secured an inheritance of provision through the Levirate law of the kinsman-redeemer. She had access to no such law as a Moabitess. She gained her inheritance through the covenant of marriage. Did she know what she stood to gain when she fell in love with Mahlon? I doubt it. Love brought her into an inheritance she could have never predicted.

Do you know what you have inherited? According to Ephesians 1, you are rich!

- In Christ, we have *every spiritual blessing.*

- We have *right standing* with Him, for we are holy and blameless in His sight.

I am convinced that if we knew how much we had, we would give more.

- We have all the *rights of a son,* for we are adopted as His sons. (I don't know about you, but I want to be adopted as a son! Remember, daughters—females—did not have any rights to an inheritance.)

- We have *redemption* through His blood and the forgiveness of sins.

- We have *wisdom and understanding.*

- We have *hope,* for we are chosen for the praise of His glory.

- We have the *promised Holy Spirit,* for we are marked in Him with a seal, guaranteeing our inheritance.

I am convinced that if we knew how much we had, we would give more.

When you know how much you are loved, you can share love more easily with others. When you understand how completely you are accepted, you are more willing to accept others. When you realize that your sins are completely forgiven, you forgive others more readily.

How did we gain this inheritance? The Bible explains it this way:

> For this reason Christ is the mediator of a new covenant, that those who are called may receive the promised eternal inheritance--now that He has died as a ransom to set them free from the sins committed under the first covenant. In the case of a will, it is necessary to prove the death of the one who made it, *because a will is in force only when somebody has died;* it never takes effect while the one who made it is living.[49]

Christ died so we would inherit eternal life and all the riches of His glory. His great love brought humanity into an inheritance we could not have possibly predicted. Like Ruth, we gain the benefits of this inheritance through making a covenant with our Redeemer. Life changing? Yes!

JOURNALING

Think about your inheritance in Christ. Are you sharing with others from your wealth?

____

____

____

____

What are some ways you can share the love, acceptance, and forgiveness He gives you with others? Think of someone specific who needs those gifts from you. List some practical ways you can give them.

____

____

____

____

____

Read Galatians 4:4-7. Copy verse 7 in the space below.

____

____

____

Turn to page 152 and pray for the _Ruth_ you know today.

PICTURE THIS
I AM

Read the Script
Exodus 3:10-15, John 18:1-6

YOU ARE

I am a writer. That is who I am and who I have always been. All my life, I have written stories, plays, and poems. I have kept a journal since I was in the third grade. My favorite books have been about girls who loved to write, like Anne in *Anne of Green Gables* and Jo in *Little Women*. If my hands were ever severely maimed, crippled, or even amputated, I would keep writing in my mind. I will write until I can no longer think because I love words.

When I was a high school freshman, I came face to face with a language that was all numbers and letters but no words, and I was lost. I could not understand it. People who spoke this language fluently tried to interpret it for me, but they could not. I diligently studied the wordless language, and my mom even hired a private tutor, but still, no understanding could penetrate my word-oriented mind. Finally, on the brink of a failing grade, I went to talk with my teacher. In frustration, he said, "You will never understand algebra. Stop trying to! You will just have to accept it."

I was trying to make sense out of something that, to me and my way of thinking, was nonsensical. In order to make a connection, I was trying to understand algebra's language of numbers and letters by wrapping them in words and concepts. It wasn't working. I had to accept algebra for what it was and work within its limits, whether or not it made sense to me.

Jesus gave us these "I AM" sayings as a way of making a connection for us between what our human minds can comprehend and who the eternal spirit of God really is. I can't explain it. God is indescribable. Just look at the life of Ruth! He is amazing! I hope you have learned through this study more of who God is. I also hope you realize that learning about Him is a lifetime journey. He is the Bread, the Light, the Door, the Good Shepherd, the Way, the Resurrection, the Life, and the True Vine. He is the Existing One, and He is so much more. Who are we?

Eventually, all persons must come face to face with God.

Picture this: We are chosen to be His reflection. Throughout our study, we see how this God of ours chose worthless wombs, corrupt capitalists, and prideful patriarchs. And He chooses us! Like Moses, we have to ask ourselves, "Who am I?" At that point, we understand it is not about who we are. It is all about who He is. He is the great I AM.

When Christ offered himself to the guards on that night in the garden, He was so confident in who He was, and who they were looking for, that He stepped forward to meet them. In the original Greek text, Christ's actual reply in verse five is "I am." (The pronoun "he" has been added by most translations for clarity.) This is what knocked the soldiers to the ground. They had come face to face with God.

Eventually, all persons must come face to face with God. They must know who He is, and they must know who they are.

One of the most important things you've done throughout this study is pray for the *Orpah* you know—an unsaved friend or family member. My friend Eddie was only twelve years old when he began praying for his dad to become a Christian. Years passed, but Eddie kept praying. When he married his wife Marla, she prayed, too. As each of their four children was born, they learned to pray for their grandpa to know the Lord. Eddie and his family knew that dying without Christ is dying without a redeemer. It is dying an eternal death.

One night, Cecil was admitted to the hospital with a very high temperature, and he was having some difficulty breathing. Eddie was there, sitting beside his dad's hospital bed. He remembers their conversation:

> I said, "Daddy, where are you in your relationship with Jesus now?" He said that he wasn't 100% sure about it. I told him that he didn't have to be 100% sure. I admitted that sometimes I have doubts, too. If he was 100% sure, that wouldn't be faith—that would be *knowing* or *fact.* If you know for sure, you don't need faith. Faith is when you don't know for sure, but you trust anyway. I assured him that if he took the amount of faith he had and gave it to God, God would make up the difference. We then prayed together and he accepted Christ into his life. He went to be with the One he trusted just a few short hours later.

So many people try to understand God and the concept of His redeeming love by using everything they know to make the connection. But no relationship with Christ can exist without faith, and for many people, that is the missing link.

By faith, you accept that Jesus Christ is who He claimed to be, the Messiah, the Son of God. And by faith, you accept who you are in Christ.

You are satisfied.

You are no longer in darkness.

You are safe.

You are called by name.

You are on course.

You are fully known.

You are a branch.

You are a reflection of Christ, made in the image of God.

You will never completely understand it. By faith, can you simply accept it?

He is. You are. Enough said.

JOURNALING

◧ Which one of the "I AM" statements has touched your heart the most during this study?

____

____

____

____

◧ Which of the "You Are" statements do you find the most difficult to accept?

____

____

____

____

◧ Turn to page 153 and pray for the *Orpah* you know today.

REALITY CHECK WITH DANYA

HIM

I watched the "popular" girls walk past me. They were laughing about something. As they walked around the corner, I knew I wasn't ever going to fit in with them. I wanted to…but I didn't want to. I had set my standards high; sometimes I wondered if they were too high, but I wanted to live my life for God, and I didn't want to compromise. They were compromising. I knew I had to live above that. I just whispered, "God, I need a friend."

He said, "I Am."

I had made another mistake. This time, I had said something I shouldn't have, and my friend was really angry with me. I apologized, and she forgave me, but I knew she was still a little angry. That night I prayed, "God, I try so hard, but I'm not perfect."

He said, "I Am."

I sat in my room, holding the phone, wanting to call my friend back. She was lost, and I was trying to talk to her about Jesus, about His love, but she wouldn't listen. She kept shutting me out. I was grieving for her inside. I couldn't reach her. I couldn't stand not being able to do anything. I cried, "God, I'm not strong enough!"

He said, "I Am."

I was listening to the music play during the worship at camp. I was surrounded by my friends, who were crying. I was on my knees, knowing I wasn't worthy of the love that was being poured upon me by my God. I just knelt there, thinking, I'm not good enough.

He said, "I Am."

Jesus is everything we could ever need, and He tells us clearly in those two, simple words. I hope that throughout this study, you've seen Him in a real and powerful way. Ruth's story is parallel to our stories. We're all lost; we're all living in a land of sin, a land that doesn't honor God for who He is. We all need a redeemer.

Boaz's story is parallel to Jesus' story. Jesus was completely willing to come and die for us. He was able to redeem us. He was willing to redeem us. He paid the full price. Now He holds out this gift of redemption to us. He showers His love down upon us. He waits with open arms for us to run to Him.

We are not worthy, and we will never be good enough; we will never be able to do anything to deserve what He's done for us. But that's the beauty of grace! He's done it all. He has forgiven us and cleansed us from our sins.

I said, "God, who am I?"

He said, "You are mine."

JOURNALING

- Take time to complete any unanswered questions and finish up any reading you need to do for Week Nine.

- Do some soul-searching about what God is teaching you. What is going on in your life, at home and with your friends?

____

____

____

____

- How can you apply the lessons you are learning?

____

____

____

____

- Are you praying Jennie's prayer? How are you seeing God answer it?

____

____

____

____

- Work on the Scripture passage you chose to memorize.

- Turn to page 154 and pray for your *Boaz*.

APPENDIX A

PRAYER: YOUR BACKSTAGE PASS

It may have seemed like a typical Saturday, but it was a day Danya had been looking forward to for months. That night, she was going to a tobyMac concert. She could not have been more excited! Then we got a call from some friends. They had backstage passes to meet tobyMac! They invited Danya to go with them. Okay, I guess she *could* be even more excited! That little piece of paper was all she needed to get backstage, get introduced, shake Toby's hand, and have her picture made with him. Very cool.

But even tobyMac would agree that a backstage "meet 'n' greet" with him is nothing compared to the unrestricted access we have to Almighty God through prayer. Just as Danya's friends held the pass that got her backstage, as Christians we are authorized to use the Name of Jesus to bring our friends into God's throne room. This special kind of prayer is called *intercession:* praying to God on behalf of someone else.

For the next nine weeks, you will be praying five prayers for five special people in your life.

Monday — Mahlon's Prayer (page 150)
Pray for someone you know who is sick, in the hospital, or undergoing cancer treatment.

Tuesday — Naomi's Prayer (page 151)
Pray for someone you know who has become embittered by circumstances of loss in her life.

Wednesday — Ruth's Prayer (page 152)
Pray for someone who is a new believer.

Thursday — Orpah's Prayer (page 153)
Pray for a lost friend or family member

Friday — Boaz's Prayer (page 154)
Pray for your future husband.

Once you have chosen the person for each prayer, write his or her name in the blanks. (Since you do not know the name of your future husband, there are no blanks on the Boaz prayer.) I suggest you read the prayer aloud, remembering that you are talking to the Lord, the Existing One.

He is real.

He is present.

He has invited you to cast every care upon Him[50] and pray on all occasions with all kinds of prayers and requests.[51] Use the space below each prayer to write down anything else God leads you to pray. You may want to leave some room for recording answers to your prayers as God demonstrates His love for these people over the next nine weeks.

Intercessory prayer is others-oriented. I'm sure these were the kinds of prayers Ruth prayed. Her life was one of worshipful service. When you take the time to intercede, you love God by serving others.

M May the words of ___________'s mouth and the thoughts of his/her heart be pleasing to You, O Lord. You are his/her strength and his/her redeemer (Psalm 19:14).

A Afraid? The Lord is ___________'s light and his/her salvation. Do not let him/her be afraid! The Lord is the strength of ___________'s life! Do not let him/her give in to fear (Psalm 27:1).

H Heal ___________, O Lord, and he/she will be healed; save ___________ and he/she will be saved, for You are the one ___________ praises. (Jeremiah 17:14)

L Let the morning bring ___________ word of Your unfailing love, for he/she has put his/her trust in You. Show him/her the way he/she should go. . . (Psalm 143:8).

O Open ___________'s eyes that he/she may see wonderful things in God's law. Do not hide Your commands from him/her (Psalm 119:18-19).

N Now I know that the Lord saves His anointed; He answers ___________ from His holy heaven with the saving power of His right hand (Psalm 20:6).

____

____

____

____

____

____

____

____

____

____

TUESDAY — NAOMI

N Now ___________ is free from the power of sin and has become a slave of God. Now he/she does those things that lead to holiness and result in eternal life (Romans 6:22).

A Afraid? The Lord is ___________'s light and his/her salvation. Do not let him/her be afraid! The Lord is the strength of ___________'s life! Do not let him/her give in to fear (Psalm 27:1).

O Open ___________'s eyes that he/she may see wonderful things in God's law. Do not hide Your commands from him/her (Psalm 119:18-19).

M May the Lord, the God of Israel, under whose wings ___________ has come to take refuge, reward him/her fully (Ruth 2:12).

I In this the love of God was manifested toward ___________, that God has sent His one and only Son into the world, that he/she might live through Him (1 John 4:9).

____

____

____

____

____

____

____

____

____

____

____

WEDNESDAY — RUTH

R Remember, Lord, those earlier days after __________ had received the light, when __________ stood his/her ground in a great contest in the face of suffering (Hebrews 10:32).

U Understanding what God has freely given __________, let him/her not receive the spirit of the world but the Spirit who is from God (1 Corinthians 2:11).

T There must not be even a hint of sexual immorality, or of any kind of impurity, or of greed, because these are improper for __________, one of God's holy people. Keep him/her from sin (Eph. 5:3).

H He will keep __________ strong to the end, I know, so that he/she will be blameless on the day of our Lord Jesus Christ (1 Corinthians 1:8).

O Open ___________'s eyes that he/she may see wonderful things in God's law. Do not hide Your commands from him/her (Psalm 119:18-19).

R Remember, Lord, those earlier days after ___________ had received the light, when ___________ stood his/her ground in a great contest in the face of suffering. (Hebrews 10:32)

P Presenting his/her body as a living sacrifice, holy and pleasing to God—may ___________ understand that this is his/her spiritual act of worship (Romans 12:1).

A Appoint Your love and faithfulness to protect ___________; may he/she be enthroned in God's presence forever (Psalm 61:7).

H Have mercy on ___________, O God, because of your unfailing love. Because of your great compassion, blot out the stain of ___________'s sins (Psalm 51:1).

Friday — Boaz

B Being anxious for nothing, may my Boaz pray about everything. Let him tell God what he needs, and thank Him for all He has done. If he does this, he will experience God's peace, which is far more wonderful than the human mind can understand (Philippians 4:6-7a).

O Open my Boaz's eyes that he may see wonderful things in God's law. Do not hide Your commands from him (Psalm 119:18-19).

A Acknowledging God in all his ways, may my Boaz trust in the Lord with all his heart and lean not on his own understanding. God will make his paths straight (Proverbs 3:5-6).

Z Zealous for God! On fire for Him and abounding in the fear and awe of His Glory! That's what I pray for my Boaz, Lord. Keep him from envying careless rebels and longing after worldliness. Keep his eyes focused on You (Proverbs 23:17).

APPENDIX B

SCRIPTURISTICS: THE NAME GAME

My friend Andrew had been trying to make it in the music business for several years. When we first met, his band was playing gigs in Knoxville and Atlanta, waiting for their big break. Andrew was convinced that one day he would meet someone who would know someone who would be his link to a recording contract. Interestingly enough, Andrew had a great "connection" already. His older sister was a well-known actress who had starred in several movies and was adored by the American public. Because of a broken relationship between the two of them, Andrew refused to take advantage of the resources her name could provide. He had been angry with her for years over a quarrel that happened one Christmas when he was a teen. He had a name—a family name—at his disposal, but pride and bitterness kept him from using it.

WHAT'S IN A NAME? Names connect us to people, places, and events. They tie us to memories, tastes, fragrances, and feelings. They evoke instant recognition of reputation and character. Names are important to God. Our Lord has many names you are already familiar with: Lord, God, Jehovah, Savior, and Father. But there are even more! The depth of God's character can only be explained by the pictures He gives of Himself through His names. Look up the Scripture references here to find the meanings behind these Hebrew names of God.

El Shaddai (Genesis 17:1) __________________________________

Jehovah-Rophe (Exodus 15:26) __________________________

Jehovah-Nissi (Exodus 17:15) __________________________

The Hebrew people gave their children names rich with meaning. Sometimes children were given the promise of future blessings in their names. Sometimes their names stated a simple truth. Some names signified the circumstances behind a child's birth. For example, Sarah named her son Isaac, meaning *laughter,* because she had laughed at the idea of a son being born to her in her old age! Rebekah named her son Esau, meaning *hairy,* because he was a hairy baby! Hannah named her son Samuel, meaning *heard of God,* because she had prayed so long to have a baby, and God finally heard her.

What about your name? Do you know the story behind it? Do you know the meaning of your name? Ask your mom or dad why you have the name you have. And if you would like to know the meaning of your name, a great Internet resource is www.behindthename.com. Record your findings below.

____

____

. Are you the kind of person who reads the credits at the end of a movie or television show? I am. I like to know the "real names" of the actors who played the characters. As the drama of Ruth unfolds, God gives us the cast of characters up front. We are introduced to the main characters, Naomi and Ruth, and to the persons in the supporting roles.

NAME	MEANING
Elimelech	my God is King
Naomi	pleasant one
Mahlon	sickly
Kilion	weakening/pining
Orpah	back of the neck
Ruth	friend
Boaz (ch. 2)	in him is strength

As you progress through your study of Ruth, you will find that each person will indeed live up to his or her name. So far, Elimelech, who was "killed off" in the first few verses of the drama, has certainly lived up to his. Whether we understand the decisions Elimelech made or not, the truth is that his God, Jehovah God of Israel, is King. He is the only one who decides upon the timing of our birth and death and who portions out our days. Elimelech may have tried to escape death from famine, but he could not flee from God, the sovereign King. Mahlon and Kilion, whose names tell us even from birth they must have been in poor health, died in Moab at young ages.

THE NAME ABOVE ALL NAMES. There is a Name that is above all other names. It is the name of Jesus. There is power in our Lord's name. There is peace, as well. The early Christians were constantly using the Name of Jesus in their conversation, their worship, and their daily interactions with other people. They were not afraid to say, "Jesus," although many times they faced persecution and suffering for it. There were countless other times when they witnessed healing and redemption just because they said His Name.

Copy Philippians 2:9-11 here.

____

____

____

____

____

____

____

As Christians, we have the benefit of His Name. Are you a name-dropper or a name-keeper? Do you offer His Name to people in need of healing? Do you use His Name yourself, taking full advantage of its power and hope? This Family Name is your connection. Like my friend Andrew, we go around in circles trying to make it on our own when Heaven's resources are at the ready, waiting on us to put down our pride and ask for help—not from a snooty big sister—but from a loving Father.

Scripture memory: Heart Work

Scripture memory is foundational to the Christian life. As we study Ruth together, choose one of these Scripture passages to memorize. God's Word will make a difference in your life!

Ruth 1:11-18

Ruth 2:5-12

Ruth 3:7-14

Ruth 4:9-17

Check out these tips for memorizing!

- Praying Jennie's prayer will keep you motivated to memorize.

- Choose a Bible version you enjoy.

- Divide the passage up into sections.

- Write and re-write the passage.

- Grab a partner and work on your passage together.

- Make a tape of yourself or a friend saying the passage. Listen to it at least twice a day.

APPENDIX C

YOU'RE ISRAELITES, AREN'T YOU?

A Fictional Retelling of the Story of Rahab the Harlot

By Dr. Ralph F. Wilson[52]

The knock at the door this evening was soft but persistent. Rahab looked up. Out the window she could see the silhouettes of two men. Customers. She was used to furtive nighttime visits by the townsmen.

Hers was a business, pure and simple—and legal, too. Oh, the wives in town shunned her, and her father had been deeply disappointed, she knew. But prostitution had brought her a good living, a house of her own, and an established place in Jericho society, albeit a less than respectable one.

The knock sounded again. Rahab opened the door and ushered the men inside.

"How may I serve you," she said with a wink, in her most seductive voice. Maybe these strangers would become regulars.

The taller one spoke in a broken and halting way. "Do you have ... a place where we could stay overnight?"

Rahab studied him closely. He was dressed like a man of the desert, but his dialect sounded vaguely Canaanite. Then she gasped.

"You're Israelites, aren't you!" It wasn't really a question or an accusation, just a statement of recognition. The man's startled expression showed she was right on the mark. Rahab rushed to the windows to shutter the room from prying eyes. What if they had been spotted?

She and all Jericho had watched as a million and a half Israelites swarmed up the Jordan and encamped at Shittim, only a dozen miles across the flat Jordan valley. When the East Jordan kingdoms of Ammon and Bashan fell to their armies, terror spread throughout the region. Jericho's king had issued a strict command to report all suspicious foreigners. The city was in a panic.

But Rahab composed herself and motioned for the men to sit as she brought them something to drink. Gone were all the seductive moves and phrases of the temptress. In their place was earnestness. When she filled their cups the second time, she sat down across from them.

"They say that your God opened up the Red Sea when He brought you out of Egypt. Is that true?"

APPENDIX C

"Oh, indeed, miss," the older one, named Salmon, answered. "I was but a small child at the time, but I remember it well. The water seemed to tower above us on the right hand and on the left."

He paused, and passed his hand down one side of his bearded face. "I can still the feel the spray on my cheeks," he said. "The wind was blowing furiously, but Mother took us children by the hand and led us straight into the wind until we were across the sea. I shall never forget it."

"Your God, what is His name?"

"Moses told us to call Him Yahweh, miss, which means 'I Am that I Am.' He always was, and always is, and always will be."

"Your Yahweh isn't some local deity, is He? I think He must be the God of the whole earth, and the heavens, too."

"Yes, miss."

Rahab was quiet and the men didn't intrude upon her silence but sipped at their cups, and whispered to each other.

"Can we stay, miss?" Salmon finally asked.

"Yes, you can stay, but I'll have to hide you. Everyone's been watching for Israelite reconnaissance parties, and you'll be killed if you're found." She paused. "I'll be killed, too, if they know I've helped you."

She got up, took their cups and put her finger over her lips. Ever so cautiously she opened the door a crack to see if anyone was in sight. All seemed quiet. Her house was perched high above the city, built across Jericho's strong inner and outer walls. She had to get the men out the door and around to the side of her house unseen, where they could climb the steps to her flat roof.

She pushed open the door and motioned for the men to follow her around the corner, up the steps. Then she pointed to the tied bundles of flax drying on her roof.

"Not my best beds," she whispered, "but the safest." The men burrowed under the flax and were invisible.

Rahab's latest business venture was to begin a cottage linen factory. Flax grew vigorously in the lush Jericho Valley. She had purchased some of this year's crop. The fresh cut plants on the rooftop would bake in sun. Then they would be soaked and beaten to loosen the long fibers in the leaves. Finally, the fibers would be combed out and woven into fine linen cloth. During the day her house could be used for textiles, while at night she would ply her accustomed trade— only until the linen business was established, she told herself.

Embrace the Reality of Ruth

Perhaps no one had seen the men, she mused. They would be extremely difficult to find even by day on a roof covered with hundreds of flax bundles. Quietly she descended the stairs and went to bed. Perhaps no one had seen them after all.

But shortly there was a banging on the door. "Open in the name of the king!"

She opened it a crack. "The king desires to see *me?*" she asked with mock innocence.

"Not you, Rahab, but those men who came to you tonight. They are Israelite spies trying to learn of our defenses. Bring them out!"

"Yes, the men came to me," she said demurely, "but I had no way of knowing they were spies. They ..." she paused for effect, "they got what they were looking for, and left, just at dusk before the city gates were closed. I don't know where they went, but if you hurry, you'll probably be able to catch them."

Lies had always been easy for Rahab. She was used to keeping men's secrets from their wives and families. Lying was part of her business, and she lied convincingly. Too convincingly, she thought. Lucrative as it was, she had grown to hate the whole dirty business. If only her textile venture would take off....

The king's men hastened away. Soon she heard the huge city gates creak open to disgorge parties of soldiers rushing east toward the fords of the Jordan to apprehend the Israelites. Rahab smiled.

She crept up the stairs to the Israelites hidden on the roof and slid under the flax herself so she could talk.

"You probably heard," she whispered. "You've been seen and the king has sent search parties to scour the Jordan for you. You can't get back across. Not now."

"Why are you helping us?" asked Salmon. "We've put your life in danger."

"I know that Yahweh, your God, has given you our land. Our people are terrified. They know how your God brought you across the Red Sea. They know what your soldiers did to Sihon and Og and their armies.

"Your Yahweh is God in heaven above and earth below. That's why I didn't turn you in. Your God will prevail, and when He does, swear to me that you will show kindness to me and my family as I have shown kindness to you. You must spare our lives—my father and mother, my sisters and brothers and their spouses and children. You must save us from death."

"Your lives will be spared, if you spare ours," Salmon assured her. "If you don't reveal our mission, we'll treat you kindly and faithfully when the Lord gives us the land."

"You must leave tonight," said Rachel. "Since my house is on the wall, you can climb down by rope. But don't head for the Jordan. Instead, hide among the caves in the mountains just west

APPENDIX C

of here. After two or three days, when they can't find you, the king's search parties will return to the city. Then it will be safe for you to cross the Jordan and go back to your camp."

"How will we recognize your house when the city is taken?" asked Salmon.

"You've seen the scarlet cord that hangs from my window," said Rahab. "That's how you knew I was a prostitute, wasn't it? When you surround the city, you'll see it hanging out the window. Look for it. You *must* look for it!"

"Just be sure you have everyone with you in the house," said Salmon. "We can't be responsible for anyone who's not inside when we take the city. But we give you our word before Yahweh, our God, that we will protect anyone who remains in the house with the scarlet cord in the window. Just don't leave the house."

Rahab nodded.

"And if you tell the authorities, we are released from our promise."

"Of course," said Rahab. "You can trust me. Your God Yahweh will prevail. I am doing this for Him—and for my family."

One after the other, the men descended the city wall using a rope. When they reached the bottom, they ran for the cover a few hundred feet from the wall.

In the light of the early dawn they could see Rahab in the window, pulling the heavy rope back up into her house, hand over hand. Then she disappeared. But in a moment she was back, and as they watched, she tied her scarlet cord in the window high above the ground.

They saw her lift a hand in final greeting, and Salmon, too, waved, before he and his colleague turned and ran for the hills.

The scarlet cord was the symbol of her profession, but as it hung there it became something more: the hope of deliverance—from war and bloodshed, but also from a life Rahab had come to hate. The scarlet cord that blew in the early morning breeze now bespoke her faith—and her salvation.

ABOUT THE AUTHOR

Rebecca Ingram Powell is a pastor's wife, a homeschooling mom, and a nationally known author and speaker. She is the author of *Baby Boot Camp: Basic Training for the First Six Weeks of Motherhood* (for new and expectant moms), *Wise Up! Experience the Power of Proverbs* and *Get Real! Embrace the Reality of Ruth* (for teen girls), and *Dig Deep: Unearthing the Treasures of Solomon's Proverbs* (for teen guys). Since 2002, Rebecca has been a monthly columnist for *ParentLife* magazine, writing the popular feature, "Mom's Life." Her articles have appeared in *HomeLife, BabyLife, The P31 Woman,* and other Christian publications and websites, including Pastors.com and Crosswalk.com. She and her husband Rich were college sweethearts and today live near Nashville, Tennessee, with their three children, Danya, David, and Derek. The Powells are members of First Baptist Church, Madison, where Rich serves bi-vocationally as Minister of Missions.

Rebecca enjoys speaking to women's groups, parents, and of course, teens. Her speaking style is loaded with humor and grounded in biblical truth, confronting real-life problems and clearly presenting practical solutions from God's Word. For more information on booking Rebecca for speaking engagements and for a complete list of topics, please visit www.rebeccapowell.com or contact Sherry@rebeccapowell.com.

Rebecca welcomes your emails and would love to hear from you! Write to:
Rebecca@rebeccapowell.com

ABOUT DANYA POWELL

Danya Powell, Rebecca's daughter, is a teenager who has been gifted by God to share the message of His grace-filled Gospel through words and music. A talented musician and composer, she plays the piano, keyboard, and guitar, and she has written over 200 songs.

She grew up singing in church and began piano lessons at the age of six. At the age of eleven, she was invited to join the teen worship band "Without Shoes" (which was based out of First Baptist Church, Madison, TN) as keyboardist. The band played together for three years, regularly leading worship at FBC. "Without Shoes" completed an album project in 2004 and opened for one of CCM artist Jessie Daniels' concerts the same year.

Danya enjoys leading worship for the youth at FBC, and she continues to accept opportunities to lead worship at area churches and youth conferences. She often accompanies her mom, leading worship at women's conferences and mother-daughter retreats.

Danya maintains a blog at www.homeschoolblogger.com/songwriter. Drop by for a visit, or send an email to Danya@rebeccapowell.com.

CREDITS

*   Names throughout this study have been changed. Pseudonyms are denoted by an asterisk (*).

1   Throughout this study, the Bible will also be referred to as God's Word and the Scriptures.

2   Joshua 2:7 The Message

3   1 John 1:9

4   Bethlehem was called Ephraim before it was called Bethlehem.

5   Also spelled Chilion.

6   Visit Steve Sawyer's website: www.art4god.com

7   Easton, Matthew George. "Entry for Goel." Easton's Bible Dictionary. 12 Nov. 2006. <http://www.biblestudytools.net/Dictionaries/EastonBibleDictionary/ebd.cgi?number=T1516>.

8   Luke 24:15-16

9   Luke 24:27

10   Jesus was betrayed by one of his own disciples, Judas. Read about it in Mark 14.

11   Luke 15:17-18a The Message

12   Isaiah 9:2a

13   Easton, Matthew George. "Entry for Jehovah." Easton's Bible Dictionary. 12 Nov. 2006. <http://www.biblestudytools.net/Dictionaries/EastonBibleDictionary/ebd.cgi?number=T2017>.

14   Ibid.

15   Proverbs 31:30

16   1 Samuel 16:7

17   John 12:6

18   Please note that Judas never fooled Jesus with his "niceness." Jesus knew his heart. In fact, Jesus had to give Judas permission to betray Him. Christ told him, "What you are about to do, do quickly" (John 13:27, NIV).

19   http://www.eeoc.gov/types/sexual_harassment.html accessed 111906.

20   Joshua 6:25 The Message

21   "Embarrassment." Wikipedia, The Free Encyclopedia. 21 Dec 2006, 08:24 UTC. Wikimedia Foundation, Inc. 9 Jan 2007 <http://en.wikipedia.org/w/index.php?title=Embarrassment&oldid=95691242>.

22   Luke 1:37 NIV

23   Liles, Dwight. "The Shepherd." Music for the Soul: Unique Resources for Healing and Recovery. 10 Dec. 2006. <http://www.musicforthesoul.org/shepherd.html>

24   Jeremiah 29:13 NIV

25   Genesis 8:6-9 NIV

26   Colbert, Don. What Would Jesus Eat? The Ultimate Program for Eating Well, Feeling Great, and Living Longer. Nashville: Thomas Nelson Publishers, 2002.

27   Deuteronomy 25:8-9

28   Campbell, Dr. Iain. "The Quest." Back Free Church of Scotland. 9 Dec. 2006
     <http://www.backfreechurch.co.uk/studies/ruth/ruth_0010.jsp>.

29   Psalm 119:105

30   John 10:3 NLT

31   Proverbs 18:24 NIV

32   Ruth 2:12

33   Campbell, Micca. "In Over My Head." Adapted. Used by permission.

34   McDowell, Josh and Dick Day. Why Wait? San Bernardino: Here's Life Publishers, 1987.

35   Philippians 2:7b-8a NIV

36   Luke 2:46b NIV

37   John 7: 3-4 NIV

38   Mark 8:32

39   John 11:4

40   Matthew 5:16

41   "Kinsman Redeemer." The Hope of Israel Baptist Mission. 26 Dec. 2006. Distributed by Hope of
     Israel Baptist Mission. Copyright 1997-2006. www.hopeofisrael.net POB 1700 Powder Springs, GA
     30127
     <http://www.hopeofisrael.net/index.php?option=com_content&task=view&id=37&Itemid=32>.

42   Ruth 4:1 NIV

43   Henry, Matthew. "Commentary on Ruth 4". Matthew Henry Complete Commentary on the Whole
     Bible. 22 Dec. 2006. <http://bible.crosswalk.com/Commentaries/MatthewHenryComplete/mhc-
     com.cgi?book=ru&chapter=004>.

44   Campbell, Dr. Iain. "The Quest." Back Free Church of Scotland. 9 Dec. 2006
     <http://www.backfreechurch.co.uk/studies/ruth/ruth_0010.jsp>.

45   Matthew 21:19 The Message

46   "Grape." Wikipedia, The Free Encyclopedia. 22 Dec 2006, 06:15 UTC. Wikimedia Foundation, Inc.
     29 Dec 2006 <http://en.wikipedia.org/w/index.php?title=Grape&oldid=95878644>.

47   1 Corinthians 1:26-28 Good News Bible

48   Ruiz, Tonya. "A Spiritual Makeover." Adapted. Used by permission. Visit Tonya's website at
     www.TonyaRuiz.com.

49   Hebrews 9:15-17 NIV

50   1 Peter 5:7 NIV

51   Ephesians 5:18 NIV

52   Copyright Ralph F. Wilson <pastor@joyfulheart.com>. All rights reserved. Used by permission.

GET REAL!

A Conference for Women and Teens

<u>Featuring Rebecca Ingram Powell</u>
(author, *Wise Up!* and *Get Real!*)

Purity

Friendships

Excellence

Wisdom

Servanthood

<u>Praise</u> and <u>Worship</u>
with teen singer/songwriter Danya Powell

<u>Special</u> <u>Purity</u> <u>Testimony</u>
by Sara Perry—who saved her first kiss for her wedding day!

<u>Four</u> <u>Sessions</u>
perfect for a two-day conference or retreat.

Visit www.rebeccapowell.com for more details!

OTHER BOOKS
BY REBECCA INGRAM POWELL

For Girls

Wise Up! Experience the Power of Proverbs is a nine-week, interactive Bible study for 6th – 9th grade girls. Covering topics of interest to the coming-of-age crowd, daily lessons deal with choices, stewardship, friends, Christ-like characteristics, and cultural issues. Heart-probing questions follow, providing an opportunity for journaling and quiet conversation with God.

For Guys

Dig Deep: Unearthing the Treasures of Solomon's Proverbs is a nine-week Bible study for guys, 7th grade and up. *Dig Deep* captivates young men with compelling stories and activities geared to a boy's journey from a wise guy to a wise man.

"Rebecca brings the Proverbs to life..." Shannon Ethridge, author

FREE Parent/Leader Guides available online at www.rebeccapowell.com

Printed in the United States
89379LV00002B/1-24/A